I0212165

As a Wolf Breathes

Poems and Prose
by
Wing Williams

within another dimension we go

one you may already know yet

have not listened to, perhaps

Copyright © 2017 by David Kelly Williams who is
Wing Williams. All rights reserved. Other than brief
passages or quotes in a newspaper, magazine, book in
reference, radio, television review, internet review, or
documentary, no part of As a Wolf Breathes may be
reproduced in any form, through any mode,
electronic or mechanical which includes recording or
photocopying or any other type of information
storage and retrieval system without written
permission from the author Wing Williams, David
Kelly Williams.

Manufactured in the United States of America

Williams, David Kelly
Williams, Wing

ISBN-13 978-0-9981127-1-8

TABLE of CONTENTS
Poems & *Prose*

Dedicated to PARIS,
as it is your love,
my love,
that is the marrow
of this book,
thank you.

As a Wolf Breathes

I.

the mountain lion

    the mountain goat

        tundra that sleeps
        beneath the snow

the red beet

    osha root in wait

        golden eagle sight

            diving osprey

    the mountain am I

    aspen shimmer

    evergreens

I am a river

I am all that sings

Follow Your Heart

The wind battered his face,
a million aqueous needles
slashing tears into particles.
Salt of the sea, salt of the soul.
He leaned into Atlas' weight,
into blanket of cosmic fall
sacrificing all torments within.
The storm of the sky
emancipated mortal burdens,
his heart-shatters scattered
west with the tempest.
There was nowhere else to go,
so, he stood and walked with
the wind past sand drummed
houses with eyelids shut.

He would follow his heart again.

A Goal

to capture not just the essence of senses
but to knock upon doors of mystery
with enough passion
with metronome fist
with pendulum breath
with zealous persistence
with tenacious pursuit of truth

in hope the enigma may answer
and invite within

to devour or host
I care not

Apparition Army

"I am a waking wolf." He sputtered.
Fresh blood trickled through
seasoned warrior teeth
brawny body sprawled long
head rested top front paws
upon bearded wheatgrass in the willows
(which had returned to the rivers).

Wolf belly thick fir matted gray wet
stench of drenched death
from breakfast, not him yet,
this final swim to his island
that would never have been
if not for him.

There was no island in '73
just murky wash of instability
too many deer, not enough nutriment.
How can riverbanks grow firm
if rain washes all away
from over scavenged terrain?

"What shall I do?" I asked the old gray sage.

Weary yellow eyes bore last into mine,
the bullet had ripped a hole in his neck
letting him wheeze these last few ardent breaths-

"Fight for a world where my son may live free.
Forgive them, forgive yourself too,

As a Wolf Breathes

but do not give up fight
'til they surrender in peace.

Restore balance
to our round green breathing gift.

We shall save the hobbles of Anasazi
where corncob and cup still lay
protected by wilderness left free
recognized aesthetic ecological
educational recreational scientific
facts we cannot drown below
rising hordes of fuel famished destroyers.

If there be no tree
what shall be left
for our sons and daughters
to breathe?

We shall fight for the red rock mesas
rising taller than man's
greed contrivances will reach
lest they be carved into new roads
leading sheep to
cement Babel towers of idolatry
erected for self-likened emperors.

Upon the phalanx of land
this phantom shall stand
my howl the guardian whisper
of eternal winds.
I shall fill the souls
of the righteous with strength
whom fight to protect the water

As a Wolf Breathes

whom fight to protect life
whom fight to protect all
breathing being's rights.

When machine beast approaches
my ghostly warrior fangs shall gnash
starting with sinful toes
'til death glares 'pon corporate neck,
apparition army shall only grow more fierce
numbers always rising 'neath
careless -not our leaders-
unless, they surrender in peace.

I am granite wall rising above valley floor.
I am shadow pacing forests thick
sucking marrow from bones of transgressors
hungry guerilla militia
eternal soul beyond tangible hold
forgiving each death with enemy throats
until, they surrender in peace."

The wolf sighed long and last,
"this is not my end young Wing,
this wolf shall run in morning mists again."

I left the king's body where it lay still,
breezes through the willows
tickled aspens beyond saddened river
their quiver one last bow
to the golden age.
Hell-rain drizzle had begun its seep.

This wolf shall not die in vain.

To Him,

a smile from her

was stronger

than any potion

of the mystics.

Jane

"They call me J.J." Jane JoVotti brushed at the air with long unadorned fingers, insinuating the smoke he blew from his cigarette encroached upon her aura.

"Who does?" Thomas Assad grinned then blew his exhaust forward again, losing the battle against headwind, blue wisps submitting to wrap about the two necks like a vain empirical scarf.

"Blow your smoke in the other direction; and they, is all whom seek my name, like yourself Mr. Assad, I do not owe anyone any specific appellation." She spoke coldly, eyes set east upon horizon, blue diamonds shadowed behind golden Bausch & Lomb Cat-Eye sunglasses avoiding his brown oculars.

He smiled at her direct demeanor, at her front facing shoulders, squared to sea, posture of a queen in dark green, afloat upon the RMS Queen Elizabeth. To Southampton, from New York City, yellow haze of heavenly wretches disintegrated into the rolling gray.

"Jane, JoVotti, it is I believe." Thomas Assad leaned forward upon the wooden bar-post, top of the three-rung railing, white, white, brown barring passengers from meddling with lifeboats or worse, death overboard. "We have met once before." His thick mustache did not hide the smile in his eyes. J.J. looked forward, east unamused. "At your wedding," his voice fished for reaction, she remained un-flinched. Short blonde hair poked out beneath her wide dark hat which fluttered like an eagle's epaulettes.

"I remember, Mr. Assad, your introduction was a bore, egotistical, and lined with business boasting. Unless you have ascended to some sort of new humble wit, then I find no reason for your smoky existence to be standing next to me." She stood satisfied, a small lift in her shoulders draped in green jacket buttoned below neck to her knees. A white turtle neck made of silk wrapped the soft skin of a woman sought by patronizing fools for wisdoms she had placed upon boats of leaves fallen with integrity, down the river into an empty end.

"Then let us sit, and enjoy the privilege slow travel provides, and please, do call me Thomas." The man wore a light gray Oscar de la Renta suit which accentuated his dark eyebrows, thick freshly trimmed mustache and salt tipped tree-trunk-hair which climbed beyond wrist cuffs rolled. He motioned to the alabaster lounge tucked from the curl of head-winds, blocked by large black and red smoke stacks that stood bold against blue sky of day with no clouds blaring as it bellowed smoke in the passing sun. An industrial fish breathing upon the Atlantic Ocean. Just blue and blue and white, brown, red, black and blue glowing starkly together, apart from their own visages.

Jane JoVotti refrained from showing amusement. A gin and tonic would truly be delightful now, though unadmitted, she turned making her way to sit and be served. She did not wait for Thomas Assad but lifted finger to the waiter boy working the top deck. Her short golden pump heels clacked the wooden slats slicing west to east. Huddle of fine grained sardines these boards were, wooden sea sliders, packed tightly upon this white minnow beneath grand circle skies, trees dead not dizzy, clack clack clack. "Tanqueray and tonic please," before Thomas could speak, before he could catch step and attempt to order for her; save him the embarrassment as whatever he chose would only get replaced by her overruling decision.

Thomas cared not but sauntered slowly her way, watching her precise affinity to independence. An estate she had inherited only by death. An estate of freedom he thought perhaps she would trade for a different kind of freedom, different from her life in Japan, in America, or in Switzerland as a widow. This woman may only partner if it meant she could remain alone in alliance, an independent leg of fortune created so vast that the price would be worth wearing the rock on her finger once more, perhaps. He finished his cigarette and joined the lady sitting now with one long cream-lit leg over the other matching her pale lips, swaying to rhythm of seascape, mimicking her heart of aspiration. She glowed like a fallen angel choosing to walk between the underworld and one above. Beautiful human of defiance, for alliance afore had washed her entire life into a set of draconian rules. Rules he believed she would only wear as choice guidelines, harp strings after war's symphony, musician shot before tightening them.

This fallen angel he had always wanted to see again, and so ensued his trip to Europe by sea not sky, for the opportunity. When she had lived in the heavens flitting by ensconced with love on lover's arm, his hand in hers, husband and wife, they the symbiotic swans on social dance floor, she had never seen him, least as nothing more than a bore, or perhaps a threat, or perhaps just another admirer, perhaps now she would see him in a new light, this a new epoch. The waiter would return soon with her drink, and then for Mr. Assad a 'saltydog' with gin, 'the breakfast refresher', as he fondly called it.

Resting himself down upon a chair next to hers, caddy cornering it a tad so his knee folded over knee mirroring her tighter image, green to gray, lady to man, gin and tonic to gin and grapefruit, gold glasses to browns, her hat to his brown hair fluttering sideways now against the grain headwinds had sculpted upon eastern faces, as they now faced south, and the sun.

"What shall we toast to?" Thomas raised his glass capturing the sun shooting fractals out of crystal.

Notes of Debussy drift from somewhere below within the floating hotel up to tingle the ears of cold drink sippers.

"Icebergs." Jane JoVotti swiftly answered his suggestion. She held her glass up to his, two crystals in the sun collide, he laughed a summer bellow, cast into the wind to fly with birds until dissipations of universal spray. And for the first time his laugh does not sting the joy of her own remark, in fact, she smiles.

Black and White

Each branch
on every tree
is blanketed with snow.
The moon is full
behind the clouds
like a lamp with
a soft white sheet over it.
Shadows
clamor cold secrets
never told
only groaned,
omens of dreams
from skeletons not asleep.

Innocence

J.D. Salinger fell in love on a day
where every ounce of weight
was displaced into ocean waves as
she splashed smiles of innocence
amidst no innocence at all.
To cure then break then mend.
Heartbroken during the war
taste of burning flesh seeps
tween shattered intentions
driving mad man pen passions
home to delirium strange
home to bathe in social apathy
to battle fakes naïve to moral
yet holding country reigns.
But she, would mend and break
then stitch him again.
The perfect moments
constructed effortlessly
-angel sitting gently beneath tree
erasing all empathy for other pains
letting tinsel of life shimmer,
laughing at all until now
at all that could rise forth
content unlike any wine swallowed.
Gratitude of the rich
seems less honest than the poor.
Love when love has no pain
is not armor for life's battles.
Lady of Esme, rudder of pen
madman music beyond kingly

As a Wolf Breathes

empty pursuits, a royal death alone
or plebeian cave dweller instead
fighting lions and snakes,
shadows of you
who attempt to tread upon
this madness of life
within my cave
within my bed,
until you look within me
with those dark eyes gifting peace,
you mend,
and for a moment
all is innocent again.

The Dreamer

Snow has weighted every wood
from sky infested albino gray fall
to evening drip and quiet calm,
pink hue tangles the passive blue
shovels at dusk rearrange the hood
soul silhouettes stand patient in wait
as sun warms fingers more every day,
tho before I see a face
I see breath leading way
by the bearers of
snow shovel weight.

It is at this time the neighbors nod
recognizing human
who must move snow too
as wolverines do
as coyote and mink
we haven't the pleasure
of a full winters sleep.

Tis a block party almost
of cars to a slant
and yellow blue red
shovels in hand
kids dragging sleds
Pa on skis
"this may be the most snow we've ever seen!"
Coffee shops full of day long
trudge sludge,

16

As a Wolf Breathes

slizzard in blizzard
drunk snowshoeing n such,

and then somewhere,
the bear smiles slow

far beneath concerns
-warm den in the snow.

'It is not I who moves the earth today,
it is I who sleeps within.'

He rests.

He dreams,

as a tree
until spring.

Guisards of the Brain

I see a mystery
when I close my eyes,
shade of gray
wearing visions of blurry animas,
theatre of old but not,
fireflies disregarded by sight
trapped within an opaque place
as a wolf breathes minstrel prayers
to those beyond transition
hunted by those who do not know
yet seek to control.
It is better to be the enigma of sound,
a wild wisp of wind
than to be enslaved
to tangible comforts of injustice.
Weakness in wishing
strength in patience
rebirth in release,
all postures of time entwined
as two blades of grass who tremble together.
Oh, the damp cloth between life and death.
No emancipation from guisards of the brain,
peaceful insomnia, torturous dreams,
silence of the moors
when the haunts do sing.

The Spaces Between

There is something I am seeking

that I yet do not know.

I feel it close watching me

within the strangers I meet

on lonely midnight streets,

spirits placed to whisper

'you do not know yet.'

This is all I know,

that I know not.

Heartstrings

Whenever I enter a tavern
or a restaurant
I look first for one thing.
Within all halls of gathering
each home I am kindly invited into,
down long streets of center towns
and hip side villages
busy pedestrian verandas
nooks of second-hand stores
lofts of hoarders
and corners of theaters
hotel lobbies with elbow bars
and always
the great stages with unlocked doors,
I seek
I yearn
I wish to find a piano,
that I may bleed my soul out into the
dissipating fissure all emotions cocoon to be,
music of mine own marrow,
invisible butterflies
emancipated
to the swirling tangle
of universe and time.

All of the Colors

When you walk down a city street
does mayhem ensure in your gorgeous wake?
cars smashing
masses of humans running into each other
fire hydrants spewing
domestic animals in stacked up apartments
howling
scratching
tearing at curtains and plaster to window panes?

When you open a book
do the pages breathe in delight
that it is your eyes that bring each word to life?
The sentences sucked up
by your supple pink lips
delightfully mesmerized by each symbol
of communication into
the wave of eternal art
in your most beautiful brain.

The trees all bow to you
for they know you are kind
they know you are the colors of the comets
shining effervescent amongst the stars.
The trees wear green for you
life walking angel twinkling in the
mirrors of puddles after rain has cleansed again
in the crystals
in each fractal
you are the rainbow bearer of heavenly hands.

As a Wolf Breathes

Does the ocean grow silent when your toes curl
upon nomadic sand dunes
pointed toward gray horizon
of western morning?

Or does it clamor louder
growling in awe of you
the tide now turning
for the sea wants to be closer to you
-as do I.

Is this why the world is not flat
for falling forever is not an acceptable
course of action for you?
Is this why my mother read to me
over and over
from the book of virtues?
Is this why music exists?
Are you music?
Are you the soul of Beethoven, Bach
Joplin, Hendrix, Marley, Aretha, Piaf,
Dylan, Miles, Astrud and King?
For you are life in gold
you are life in green
you are life in black
for you are everything.

Silent Observer

The silence of his hall had fallen again to the midnight rompers of mountain new year celebration. Only for a few hours each day would this purgatory cell share his apparitional cloak of silence. Wooden walls groaned slowly in the wind. The train rumbled by clacking again. A bear checked the metal trash bin to see if the barkeep had cared or not to lock the waste before old-Toyota-crawl home deep into gulch down long dirt road. Between the last drunk, last sweep and cocaine bump until the baker came in and put on the morning's first pot of coffee, only then would this wooden prison be his to sing within. No face to look through his wistful-once until morning come, no tobacco lipped mutt owner to step on invisible foot, no dame to care not, no warm pulsing reminders of mortality, just him and the echo of mountain growl. These hours of silence he treasured, for mostly he must observe the ever-changing living. Silently he would glide, occasionally knocking a pint glass to the floor, always intentionally. Lo the eternal torture of unobserved silence! Western winds whirled his ethereal screams into train shrieks, words dripped too saturated by oxygens to be heard, unless, all was still. Only in the silence would the empty walls echo his moan.

It was his 77th new year's celebration here in the hall of stomp. In came the hippies with hair long,

the bikers with trucks tonight, the gulch dwellers
laden in leather, gold coins in deerskin satchels
hanging by long bladed knives with bone handles,
ladies fine with oxen grips and shoulders bare
above armpit hair and twirling home patched
skirts with wool leggings holding whiskey flasks
and cash from selling beaver hats, and the
musicians from pickers to stage travelers with
guitars and basses and mandolins and banjos and
any other box with some sort of strings attached,
the bearded, the dreaded, the bald, the old with
generations of kids in tow, the commune families
wearing wreaths, the lone ranger who only sings
on this one night of new year celebration, the
loggers, the wild burghers of Ward,
swashbuckling blacksmiths and stone-masons all
keen in the art of sword, the drifters of the
continental, miners of Eldora silent until today,
all chromatic folk of the high country enter the
door of the Stage Stop Saloon, to tear down the
silence of time again, to dance upon the wooden
floorboards above and drink the wells dry below.

He paced his domain watching it fill with the
radicals of today, with governments men retired
to wash city sins clean high up in the mountains,
trading their suits and ties in for an axe and
overalls many years ago, with artists who study
stars and write prophetic prose on lodgepole bark,
do-not-mess-with-me's now smiling for tonight
all laces were laced and all boots snow shined
until later when laces get ripped in bathrooms and
boots get strewn by woodstoves aglow.

"Up here the richest man is the one with the most firewood." Geno tells a flatlander wide eyed at the mountain sinew circus developing around their clean pressed clothes. "I ain't even seen a damn shirt like this before," picking with calloused flattened fingers missing two finger-nails at the crispness of factory filth draping smooth-faced city-slick. Flatlander smiles red as his wife clutches his soft arm tighter, he winces a bit at her tightened worry, at Geno's beaming breath. Geno pats the man's shoulder heartily, enough to make him wobble and resettle his stance then smile. Who could not help but smile with Geno?

Around and around the Stage Stop flit the ghost. Wooden prison walls he can never escape, save for deck up on the second floor, only there could he shimmer in western winds pouring off the continental divide ripping through Rollins Pass down gulch as train charges east towards Denver. He now but the fog of gaseous mutt smoke twisting through white grey limbs, matter of destiny no longer. He now but a few memories faded and the bone marrow chills to strangers.

Downstairs, the main bar, long and flat against tall glass mirrors, wore shelves that held bottles that begot winter burrowed mammals drunk before returning to folds beneath the snow. Each stool now wore the dress of ladies and Carharts, friends layered in long sleeves crammed in-between. Brothers of cousin's long time unseen reach for whiskeys and beers and the occasional wine pour. Snow dragged in by boots and weathered hems now lay as fading mirrors, puddles trampled by the bustle, evaporating with footprints up the stairs to left of long bar turning upward twice counter clockwise to pour the ascenders 'pon hall of dance, floor of wooden bounce, tree planks once sun worshippers now horizontal beams wearing circular scuffs. The grain never wore away from its truth, and thus the ghost would only pace parallel or perpendicular to the boards he counted each year. Pale parallelogram thing sliding through the breathes of humans spinning, around and around.

They could feel him pass through though most too inebriated to consider the gasp or irregular heartbeat or cold shiver down spine or hair of wrist ripple to toe, but each felt him and drank again and stomped wilder to the grassy sauce of fiddles pluck and bow draw. Drums lit the air with a beat of marvelous acquaintance, smoke sidling in through the door to deck rarely closed, always swinging back n forth letting legs of deerskin in to let hems of purple home-dyed laces out.

He floated through the glass panes too foggy to see through out to his deck and limit of eternal reach. From basement to deck, from the kitchen to perimeter dining room walk, he would never sleep, only pace around the beam that held the rope that his breathing neck hung its last breath. For he too once had a body like these dancers of new year come, he too wore the drape of never shave and never replace, only mend and repair and re-wear year after year until the animal fits the human like one's own skin.

The Man Over There

cold rain falls slight
hanging,
oceanside behavior
it emulates

in mist like, he sits
hungry
bare hands pulled into sleeves
lonely shivers

those who walk by
hurry on
hood over head
drier than he

perhaps they don't see
him there
statue town fixture
who always stares

through desiccated tears
an empty sigh
only the mist like rain
listens

Child Sight
(for Dudley's Bookstore & Café)

To exit café
one must pull not push
upon red door
which retains
winter heat from
absconding.

No sign indicating
this simple method,
incurring many an
escapee to do so
with abashed shake
of bobble head.

Some stubborn fools
will not surrender
impulse that
the way they came in
must be,
the same to get out.

Another door thrust,
heavens it is stuck!
No free instructions
common sense not enough,
one more shove, ah…
gentle pull I must.

Lawyer man with books

As a Wolf Breathes

of knowledge
discovers
this rouge wood,
to be only one
of his problems.

Lady in fur,
stubborn rock
not water
mindful of pendulum,
is not
what she offers.

A gaggle of teenagers
almost kicks it down
laughing
sneezing
colts to pursue
fillies in town.

Then along comes
a little one
shorter than the handle
she pauses to consider,
an exit successful,
sipping on hot chocolate
blooming brain remembers,
as she entered café
mother pushed red door away,
so, without slightest nudge
she pulls with her finger
skips into crisp air
mind unencumbered.

Spring Celebration

Celebration of rising spring,
sun rises earlier,
coffee cools not as quick
lavender wisps of tomorrow's kiss
wrap around warmer fingertips.

Those two robins now twice the size
from when frozen ground
inhibited earthworm rise,
bears circumnavigate town
bold on sloppy hobo
midnight leftovers no mo'.

Star friend travelers return
as we stand upright in eternal tilt
working the dirt inducing
her sustenance to slip
out of midnight lover's silk.

Dancing howls around rising pyre
savage paints of earthly mire,
the season of skin now begins!

-chanting shimmer in Aspen winds-

Enlightened eyes
seek horizon brighter,
shedding the dead
of melancholy's dim.

The Swans

Annular Vs of luminous sparkles
wake of lover's waltz – open triangles
contriving figure-eights that undulate
star diamonds to shore, ripples dissipate.

All hail the Trumpeter Queen & her King
on midnight dance in ballroom of moonbeams
his long white bow to her pristine graces
passion the strongest in secret places.

Tango of the two a lifelong amour
coquetry on glass of eternal lure
grandiloquent speeches worshiping her
sonorous song of swan reminding her,

there are no plumes milkier than yours dear
obsidian bill, none exists more fair
cygnet mother, protector of our glides
your pen beauty eternal in my eyes.

To his praise she spans resplendent feathers
alerion lovers - to the other
they've tangled their necks – two galleons afloat
to become one wed alabaster boat.

The Dive

out of breath from the climb
steep shale fall
scree uphill wade
-you must lean into her
below water travels onward
gentle clamor where rock
interrupts flow in front of
old juniper men who've seen
many snowfalls many snowmelts
river high carving curves into mud
clamor more when river low
autumn weary
from summers quench-
today though
with back against cliff
atop scree fall upon river throne
two bald eagles hunt higher above
gray shower of snow occasional
against a dimmer sun
the eagles hang as if on
heavenly strings
angel fingers orchestrating suspension
-until
the dive

Ye Ol Hobo

I tip my hat to the runaways,
to the broken hearted
fast feet shadow sleepers,
mountain goats drinking
nomadic ecstasy to cope.
I tip my cap to the ol lonely jazz cats
breaking down tobacco butts
for one long smoke at last
highway drifters who've decided art
will give their souls the rest
'tween muddy piss flaps,
truck stops n mobile does
keepin on down the long dark groove,
in confusion waking 'neath alien red lights
slinkin out passenger side or jumpin out the back
crust from Oklahoma still in the eyes
shining now
at further west paradise.
Here is a warmer kinder shore
here the trees breath taller reaching for more
here the guitar can happier sing
from the Rockies to Sierra – north to Cascades!
Ah the drier breeze.
Ah the wolverines!
Marble Mountain Wilderness
no more eastern trench feet!
I tip the ol dirty stained blue atop head
for so long
hiking mountain to mountain
wondering where I belong,

As a Wolf Breathes

I tip it to the long-bearded bikers
growling by in both lanes
to gypsy caravans, to thumbs for busses,
hippies in Westfalia's, to ye ol hobo
walkin in the rain.

There's an old man you may meet
out on the road,
age 110 if you believe what your told
Patch the Elder, squintin outa one sphere
with no patch where other globe should go.
He'll spit in your eye
lean closer if you pull back
he's got that stinkin wisdom
outa rotten cavity cracks.

-You can't ride em trains
like when I was your age –
damn internet electronics – demon captains –
invisible cancer of the plains.
Gimmi the sheriff rappin on boxcars
who can only beat your blood
til you've run outa the yard.
They chased me in Amarillo
threw me in the hole in Denver
then 50 STP pack rats in one boxcar to San Jose!
You know the STP?

-Yee I know the STP, I lived in Nederland man!
Sagittarius Taurus Pisces
Serenity Tranquility Peace
Sex Type Thing

-Naw (he spat)

As a Wolf Breathes

Stuff the Pigs man…
stuff the pigs….
San Jose kid (he got closer still)
killed a man that night
but that is your right
when it's the knife or your life.
If you go to San Jose, walk in, walk out.

He grunted n swayed, frothed smoking lips now
smacked shut.

Ol Patch the elder looked Northeast
one eye set upon the horizon,
his other eye now dirt
white whiskers twitching – nose black drip –
bags and folds, skin tucked into
warm still breathing flesh
a brain in a head mostly bald,
spirit in a rucksack of the never-ending road.

Dusk

Just before the sun drips
below mountain horizon,
light lingers
in mirror of river.

Ripples dissipated,
geese have fought,
ducks have cleaned
necks tucked into plumes now
for muddy bank rest
each with a mate
except for one lonely male
having lost the contest – today.

Golden glass grows gray-blue,
evening songs include
the yip of coyote
hum of hive discussing tomorrow's chores
whippoorwill lovers opening evening's door.

Last orange on willows closes its eyes,
as day travels away,
night draws nigh.

Whiskey on an Empty Stomach

The next morning
hands shake a good bit
melancholy contemplation
heavy brain blankets,
python on bones
pulses rapid lava gas
incinerating good;
a fog remains
whole memory
no longer breathing
drifted into dreams
-torrid tortures
battles in mind spilled
onto human ground.
Behind last trash bin
down darkest alley
in grease drip
of forgotten filth
I scrape my fingernails
and lick all the poison
my soul can repulse.

The birds still sing
like yesterday
the sky a gentle blue,

if the whiskey kills me

the flowers will still bloom.

The Wretched Man

They threw him to the ground into a puddle of fresh rain mixed with city sole shoe trudge. His chin did not yet hurt, his neck neither, nor his head, wrist or ribs. All he felt, as murk filled his nose's right cavern, as his vision bloody returned to a gray horizontal world, was the beating pain of misguided passion.

Sure, he had been drinking bourbon on a tortured heart. Sure, he accused the bartender of stealing his debit-card, then thrown a shot glass at the blond pale thief. He surely threw fists at tall men dragging him out of the loud reverberating tavern. And sure, he had burst back into the den barreling straight to the old piano standing alone in dark corner and wailed upon the ivory as only a drunk bourbon man can, when no one will listen. The DJ throttled up the heat, the tall men removed his sweaty frothing body with more disciplinary force.

'Not in this land,' he thought, picking himself up by concaved palms. Vehemence faded into tired heavy shame. He stood beneath their door-barring glares, cleaned out each eye with middle fingers and turned walking slowly in mist lighting a cigarette as tears meandered down each cheek. 'Perhaps not in any land do I exist. Bound by a darkness I cannot escape. But this is not the way, I do know. Bourbon whilst melancholy, I never should have...' Saturated socks in boots of tired seams led him onward avoiding the city lights, tripping over hobos in parks asleep beneath fences he jumped. His hands now sliced and red by the arrogance bourbon wears.

One hobo cursed at his too-close shuffle. Drunken retorts were exchanged, guilt became the wretched man's shadow as he sunk into a bench bathed in one light alone by weary waters of consumerism. Three cigarettes he had smoked since this last social representation of himself, so here on the bench by the water that invited heavy immersion, sirens of gentler depths seducing his tired brain, he lit a fourth. Smoke ascended to rafters wearing pigeons somewhere, to seep within windows of lovers who forgave others and themselves as a practice. He cursed the satisfied sleepers and yearned for more booze.

The water before him mesmerized all tingles of sanity. It melted his tendril shards that waved as lung tubes unconnected to life into a molten batter of obsidian. He stood up from easement of leg use and wobbled upon the edge of a crumbled intentional dive into peace. All that had weighed choked his mind. Living serpents encouraged death, cancerous harm to once kinder intentions.

The shuffle of another draped in black, for the night consumes all colors, sidled behind pausing once to look upon the man standing on river's edge. The ghostly glide continued on into midnight's after-hour without a mutter nor concern.

"No, this is not the way." The wretched man croaked beneath impaired breath. He fell backwards upon the cool cigarette butt littered earth away from the depths of mortal reprieve. "No, this is not the way" he mourned.

First Breakfast

after meditating
top desert rock crop
east mother heat now glinting child's eye
on return to camp observed dry-land manna
prickly pear cactus for breakfast
the pad the petals the pear
slice it into many
pink baby elephant ear
bloody juvenile tuna
pull the prickers out
sliver scoop knife in between
oooh juicy groove!

dirt dweller trekking to springs
sponge dripping beard

red rising sun

calloused feet patient

soul savoring the still

green mojave rattlers wake
creep into the gold

Instructions

climb a mountain alone
apply jewel weed to poison ivy
dandelions – cattails – nettle – elderberry
food and medicine
sleep on the dirt
learn the stars
listen to birds -they are messengers
never leave trash in the woods – ever
talk to bears calmly
aspen bark milky film is spf 5
sleep on eastern facing slope
awake with sunrise
carry embers in mushrooms
manzanita not pine
shit 200 ft from water
dig a hole then bury it
red fox is watching you

Ripples of the Underworld

the dirt on cheek is warmer
than yesterday
little green needles
just taller than ants
entwine with beard
like lover's legs
rising from the brown
no longer frozen ground

souls of so many

star counts

sand gems of each
woman and man
that have been
and shall be again
envelope
breathing through molecules
now flesh
ripples of the underworld

Princesa

As I arrive
the first thing I notice
upon deck full of mirth,
before tables of candy colors
island dancer tween no walls
all windows unencumbered
with suspended flowers
pinks purples white
sunset droplets clinging to earth
disguised as pastel petals,
it is she I see,
angel of laughter
woman of grace conducting this painting
floating above the floor
with antelope precision
lioness demeanor
royal posture
and her father's smile.
This exquisite lady of melody more
causes my heart to hum,
as if it a caterpillar
transforming into a butterfly.

The Beginning

Pay no mind to the sun
to the beginning of a day
or the end.
Wrap the universe into
one long kiss
rolling tongues
until all flesh is basked
in batter of seduction.
Blades of grass paint
sweat drip skins neath
straw hat shade for lips,
petrichor brushes
entwine with hair
crimped from moon-long grasps
wrapped to abolish
all space between
carnelian tangle
of no hour glass
caressing swan's
graceful arch
cartilage nibbles
on nirvana pilgrimage
bathing in wet
of lovers unleashed.

Milk

chalcedony marvel
herbaceous lips

feathers erotic
catalyst

euphonious bouquet
blue anamnesis

carnelian swim
dawn's grey mist

Gravel Bleed

from the Valley of Wind
to the Alabama Hills
to climb up over crest tallest way
gravel bleed 'n sun long stings
highway paradises in between,
lean against rucksack
shimmer with trees while
writing songs 'n
lighting smokes low slink
into metal jitter roadway shake,
white wisps whoosh far
into view of mother mountain
where breakfast was eaten
yesterday

sew up the rips
behold twilight lashes
deep into the east
lay beneath stars singing
moonbeam heart scars

winding serpent slithers
quickly beneath

The Return

Four nights in Portland was enough.

Kind weary eyes agree tacitly

>midst whirl of wind
blowing city sins
savage chaff
through our bodies
leaves
rotting
in fences
til hurricane
cleanses.

East fast down 84.

Columbia carpet leading us

>to wilderness door
to The Bridge of the Gods
then north high
into grizzly fog
into glacial carved sanctuaries
where eagles
shall harvest
venomous snakes
from mine soul.

Forgiveness & Rebirth beneath turpentine
pillars.

Beneath the Street

I walk to the store with little in my pocket
only what I need, plus cigarettes.
The bills have been managed,
got drunk two nights ago
to celebrate living on little
to celebrate being alive,
even if it means
being dirty and broke 'til tomorrow.
Under the highway – in piss shit alley –
where the puddles don't evaporate away
just freeze, melt,
then cling to shoes and jeans
-she sits.
Crumpled faded feathers
withered within once blue jacket
head between legs skinnier
than rolled up yoga mat
finger nails black – shaking – tearing – digging
into blond matted brain.
She does not look up as I walk by.

At the store I feel so heavy,
too much money
too much clean
it is her stench and pain I want to bathe in
to bear it all – for her to be clean.
I buy my cigarettes,
two sandwiches instead of one
two orange juices
and one dark chocolate raspberry bar.

As a Wolf Breathes

Back beneath the highway she still sits.
When I stop,
she now looks up -alone and afraid.
I hold out the food and sit down next to her,
we slowly eat
cry
then smile.

The World's Kindest Crescendo

Tree with arms to the heavens she is.
Torso twist divine,
leg slight over other,
hips don patterned silks effervescent,
breasts bare to tonic hum of wind,
elysian leaves tangle drifting clouds,
shimmering hair greets celestial streams,
vine of ascension weaves floral crown.
She is the world's kindest crescendo.
This Queen of Sacred smiles with
toes outstretched on soiled chest
rooting sole of soul in petrichor heart.
She sings
she strengthens
she dances.
Curl's golden penumbra bounce
as whisper through flower petal lips
whistling wellspring of amaranthine beauty;
she gathers atomic charms and creates
new moons
new words
new tenderness.
She tucks me into her velvet shade
beneath lioness wings
where at long last,
I sleep in peace.

Green Flutter

we refined our discussion
to details of pure existence

to the drape of the world

tinseled relaxation

effortless peace

symbiotic companionship
with gravity

wind sleuths
graze our skin and compose
green flutter within

Dear Mother

It may have been
many moons
since we saw each other last.
The winds I feel must climb
many mountains to reach you,
they must travel the bladed tawny plains;
the sun may shine upon you each day
before it warms my forehead
and yet, I always feel you.
I am attached to you eternally,
as your son.
I still hear you play piano
as I fall asleep.
I breathe, because of your love.
No matter our distance,
no matter where I rest my head,
I shall always thank God for you.
I shall always love you my mother dear.

Between Rain Drops

out window I hang
for midnight cigarette

fingers reach for clouds release
falling beyond shingled eaves

smoke escaped
from cylinder cell

rises

to join the other
phantoms of nocturnal life

they exist between rain drops
never getting wet

listening to whispered words
of this ardent silhouette

Save the Earth

For the focus,
must be a greater tomorrow,
within today's urgency of action.
To live only for today yields
mortal unleavened bliss.
To live today intentionally
as building block of love
as step or pivot towards peace
as lattice of sustenance
as fist of slavery demolition
as warriors to save the earth,
then all this our children
too shall pursue passionately.
Tsunamis of hatred ally
with wildfire injustices
devouring life as terra grimaces,
sweating breaths of child deaths
by hand of child
given the sword of murder
from proud predecessors.

The pit of despair is not
as far below the surface
as we may like to think.

Tinseled by glittery trinkets
selling ideas so simple as fantasy,
sleuths slither disguised
as progression and comfort.
Against these monstrous

As a Wolf Breathes

corporate killers,
slash tentacles 'til heart is reached,
against prejudicial armies
oozing dissension and sin,
stand as ocean cliffs of love
righteously vehement
intolerant to hatred,
eyes alive with brain aware
for opportunities of unbiased kindness.
Create art and renewable energies,
challenge rules that demote individuality,
do not participate in slavery,
civil disobedience is your right
your expectation as citizen,
we not the sheep.
We the bearers of soul torch
the givers of sharpened life,
our influence on the future
is our daily responsibility.

To save the earth,
we must save the children.

April 10

Today is a powerful day.
Life lived intentionally.
Sprouting Grass Moon
anniversary of facing fears,
walk boldly into unknowns.
Wisdom diamonds veiled
within onyx time.

April 10 – eyes young
soul fervent,
cold mountains bathe
in blue mist
into the wild
on pilgrimage to Maine.
Walk of the leaf.
Ear of Tears.

April 10 – eyes older
nectar overflows
alone to walk
desert and mountains
Mexico to Canada.
Spring of Rattlesnake.
Summer of Sierra.
Autumn of Cascades.

April 10 – to Hawaii
mystery cloaked in
midnight rains
-pain to heal pain.

As a Wolf Breathes

April 10 – rise in Carolina
drive to Oregon.
Soul of sun travel,
nocturnal peace exists
in the west.
It will be nix unless we do.

Oh, each and every April 10
I lift my chin and strive again.
For the out of reach
is not so
if our focus and fight is pure and tenacious.

Today -celebrate, love honestly,
river flowing forward
in green mountain breath.
Allegro feet dive
into untrodden valleys of marvel again.
Squeeze the fruit – drink the juice.

Pink Moon

Great Grey Owl

Juniper King

Wolverine

Pink Moon

Feet buried in tidal sand
water draws against,
the world moves but I do not,
moon penetrates
in last moments of wax
eruption to occur soon
but not yet,
my raucous stand as
superhero comet across idea
chokes on stealthy sand sleuths
grit between teeth
odd untamable crunch
I spit I curse I think not of…
Universe pulsing breath entices
my pace, my angst
my heartaches
my wrath subdued,
heart artifacts
moon-seep seduction
vanilla moldavite zephyrs.
Van Gogh looked aside
seedling breezed by
his paintbrush laid
nimble fairy fingers
unscathed by time;
he always saw the beauty
that flies away,
as I do,
as too does the moon.

Love Affair

I am having a love affair.
It is dark and dangerous
in a -you should build a lighthouse here-
apparition captain whisper.
My tongue seeks each droplet
sap of her squeeze
nectar to the thirsty insatiable desire
I carry for the heartbeats
for the trees
for the wind
for you.
I am having a love affair
with this entire ferocious world.

Beauty wears an ugly mask at times
and so became my eternal dive
into pain we all wear
'neath social calisthenics
which breed horrors
which humans create.
How to properly serve
the earth 'pon we all were birthed? -perhaps.
I a vessel overflowing with love
for hope within the ash,
I a seeker of buds green and fresh
penetrating grounds once suppressed.

Father's Road

Up in the plains tween clouds and moons
Bar Headed flight o'er Himalayan crests
across each long deep sparkled blue
into new sunrises and old sunsets
mountain vines tangle spinning sphere
electric lights web the vast horizon
there – Captain Calm keeps flying on
pointing to land perhaps his son now treads.

Down in Rhododendron tunnel
cooking dinner by flame in jungle rain
mud clad boy sits low, huddled to
fire unseen beneath the thick cotton greys
earth tone tarp shields him from sharp wind
vision annulled here in green southern grove,
he lifts face t'wards wet white heavens
drenched by the drip of his father's road.

Bear Pagan

Bear Pagan sat on a plastic bench carefully turning the dry papery leaf in his fingers. He double checked to make sure no one else could see what he held. What an odd specimen this is, what did the old man mean? Beyond the dirt of alley sleep dissatisfaction, beyond the grunt of frothing lips, like the bold rabid racoon shot at noon yesterday, (one less racoon in the world, numbers down to probably less than 100, legal to kill on sight, frothing or not), beyond the old man's stink his words held weight for young Bear Pagan.

"Do you know what your name means boy?" the old man spat stopping Bear on his walk home from school, first day of class, first day of 6th grade, the name BEAR in red marker on white sticker still clinging to day-long worn t-shirt over young melancholy heart.

Of course, he knew, his aunt had told him repeatedly as a boy since she had adopted him after his parent's disappearance, death by The Forest, up on Mount Cascadia, bodies never recovered in the tangled murk, for who would go in and bring them out? No one ever returned from The Forest. He had been only 4 years of age when this befell, so his visions in brain remained limited. He remembered his mother's hair, how she wore it in long braids down her back, when she did not the breeze would flutter silky brown strands into his mouth as she sang him to sleep. He would pull them out and turn the other way, she would laugh and whip her hair around like a great tree, for this is what she called herself. Bear had only seen pictures of trees she had drawn. A live tree, it must be such a beautiful thing.

All he knew was what his aunt would tell him. Aunt Melania always spoke coldly it seemed, perhaps even scared, but he knew she must be burdened, to lose her sister, to support her nephew Bear. The day the men came and told him his parents would never return, they took all belongings, pictures, clothes they had owned. For this is what you do when someone dies, eliminate memory, it is weak to hold on. Bear often felt the guilt of this weakness, his sinful sentimentality. One scarf his mother owned he had kept and hidden safely away for the last 7 years. Faded greens, blues, white, gray, and black elephants and orange, red, yellow and purple giraffes all marched within a maze of patterns, he would lay it out full when Aunt Melania was not home and stare at the weird creatures upon it. From what imagination had these strange things come? The name elephant, giraffe, still clung to mind's dark corners as cobwebs in a forgotten barn. He believed the wide one with big ears to be the elephant.

Her ancestrally drilled information was all he repeated, whenever asked what his name meant, usually from a tone of condescension. Like a broken record, a saying he did not comprehend, he stated "sure do sir, to support, to produce, to remain firm against all weight. I am the strength and man of my family, I may be just a boy to you, but I am my aunts only son, well nephew, but I am the support, her duty to bear, I am strength, and maybe her own weight... to bear..." Bear's voiced trailed off to a lonesome place.

"Uh huh." The old man grunted, swayed in his rusty alcohol dried baggy skin, "you may think that, but it is not so. Your father and mother did not name you Bear after a support beam kid, or even for strength the way you think it." For a second the old man wore a sympathetic smile. "Say kid what is your last name?"

Bear toed at the clean asphalt earth. He looked up into the old man eye's, black, with scars across his face, where the regulators had beaten him. A tough life for the beggars, poets and musicians of the streets, often seen getting beaten for being too dirty. "Pagan." He replied timidly. This name was never received well, conversations would end, other kids would avoid him, some daring few threw rocks, which too was a sin, to rearrange, rocks were for décor and erecting great monoliths to the great country of ONE (One Natural Entity.)

The boy angered at this suggestion, that this alley trash, this beggar of money would assume to know why or why not his parents had named him Bear. He stepped back unnerved, but the old man snapped out of his gentleness spewing stench and myth, striding forward aggressively. Young Bear jumped back to street edge, where cars and finely clothed citizens and surely the machine guards would not let him become maimed. 'The cleanest streets in the world they say, then what is this bum doing here?'

"Have you ever heard of, a bear? A BEAR! The old man roared jumping at the boy, his hairy arms waving about like a giant erratic moth, dust and stench unpleasing wafted into young Bear's face. He stepped back disgusted and slightly confused. "A BEAR boy, was the king of the land, walked on all fours like a racoon, hunched forward, giant paws, giant claws, he could kill a man with one swipe, knock his head right off, he could stand on his hind legs like we do, and far above he, or she, would tower, thick and brown and mean as lightening, or," the ol man started to calm down, soften his tone, "or as sweet as a curious dog, if you listened to them right…" his voice trailed off into alley murky breeze.

Bear had never heard of a bear, he did not know that they were brown, black, white, blonde, shaggy, kind, he had not lived long enough, nor had the bears. The last bear died 20 years before his birth, skinny and malnourished, broken hearted and caged, the great species of Ursidae no more. Natural history was not taught in schools, for it was pagan, not conducive to human's dominance. No room for the bears, little room for birds or dogs, nearly end of the line for even racoons. All the land was covered by homo

66

sapiens and the objects they'd built. Rails, roads, transportation in constant motion, oxygen factories, food factories, walkways 1,000 feet up connecting each tower of the land-covered sky from one ocean to another, mountains terraced or bulldozed flat, rivers clogged and rerouted, trees all destroyed. Here in this land there is no room for anything that breathes except for the almighty human.

Bear could not run away, his curiosity at this unpleasant man's tales engaged him more than most who spoke. This man did the very opposite of the others, he wanted to talk to Bear, to tell him things, not to turn his back and shun the boy. The filth and stench became less so to Bear, now he wanted to know more, what is this bear, this creature he speaks of? Though told through saliva and dirty scars, perhaps this old man was telling him of something true.

Bear spoke boldly now. "Have you ever seen a bear?" He asked the man. But the man did not speak. He looked down kindly upon the boy and slowly reached into the folds of his layers. Out he pulled a tan fabric unknown to Bear.

"This is leather," he spoke, "the hide of an animal." Looking both ways to make sure no regulators were observing the two, he opened the leather as a book folded into three and turned his back to Bear, no-one but the crow atop the alley trash could see what was held within. The man turned again to the boy who stood there still, straight, engaged, dirty blonde hair disheveled upon sweat of forehead, he slipped the leather back into his folds and held out his hand with palm to the ground towards the boy. "Put out your hand." He spoke gently. Young Bear obeyed. The man then placed his large rough dark hand upon that of Bear's. Weather and wisdom encompassed white smooth naivety. He placed a maple leaf, now dead, dry and brittle, edges missing, delicately into Bear's palm.

The boy held the leaf carefully aware of its holiness, and then quickly slapped his other hand over too knowing the danger of possessing such a thing. He looked up to thank the old man, to ask him his name, to ask him so many questions, but the soothsayer had already turned and disappeared into the stench of in-between.

Eternal Surfer

Trying to process all this confusion
between dreams and awake
velvet sheen of unbridled silk
where fingernail scrapes take place
between moral and ideal
driven to delirium
freed from parameters
toss the stone and never watch the ripples?
Not I.
Eternal surfer
of rising figure eights
for in those dimensions
your eyes sing tacit songs
that leak onto tangible midnight streets
into colossal kisses
between definitions
puddles of all paint
of all colors
our own kaleidoscope kingdom,
here, no reason or rule must live.

Older Youth

Fire scent lingers
in tumble weed hair
grey smear still beds in chest
ash of yesterday
beneath lines of heavy lay,
morning mirror crumpled
in day past truths
night songs
foreshadow
an older youth.
I did not like coffee
as a boy,
I did not treat my heart
as a toy,
so now
as I drink black sludge glue
tightening seams loosened
from my own faults,
I wash off yesterday,
turn on a lil jazz
let pain yeast breathe
eager for wisdom bread
-sustenance of an older youth.

Tempest

My heart is a tempest
destroying
all exorbitant bridges
all cabins on weak foundations
spitting hail upon woes
piercing perhaps with fire
winds of god-pace
eliminate chaff
seeking cauldron of love
that tumbles not over.

I forge a lighthouse
out of all the rocks hurled
by my own mistakes.

Gluttony

poison on poison on poison

even food will kill you

sustenance too much – is not

health is only length of chapter
and caliber, I suppose

egotistical
righteous
religion

until the next chapter,

which 'ain't a bad thing,' said the butterfly.

Funny Bones

Funny bones are not funny
instead, when wacked,
minor momentary
needles of torture.
The initial bop ain't too much
a second thought
of once satisfied elbow
not burning in rot,
'til the fire creeps in
lava cancer overtaking
all ambidextery.
No longer
can elbow merely slighted,
hold up the arm and
act like nothing has begun.
Little tap upon
corner surface just so
has undone all action of limb,
opposite of strong non-slighted right,
hanging limp
flopping about like prehistoric gimp
after a tussle with sabered lion.
It is the burn I shall not think about,
just let it hang
millions of piranhas chewing on me
in ticklish warm
non-childlike glee
I curse, I laugh,
Blast!
I've hit my funny bone.

Balance

the winds have travelled onward
        to new battle grounds
only the slowest ones still pass thru
        harmless wisps tickle nose hairs
zephyr messages from mountains
        agree with spring
badgers east shall taste
        this ribbon soon
-but wait
there is a sudden shift
the sunshine birdsong dims
yellows blue gray grayer black
the sun now a billion trillion pebbles of hail
sky corrosion beating black pulse
        onto forehead
        melatonin shocked
        weakened by winter hibernations
-she calms
the yellow warmth returns
zephyrs whisper
-for now

Evening Lethargy

Sun beam not as acute
softer into eyes full
of day-long soak.

Water after chute -ease
slow and wide
creeping across flat land.

Song of hatchlings fed
announces crickets
who shall come.

Man in overalls walks slow,
horse and plow retired
until tomorrow.

"How was your day?"
she asks, removing
corn from husks.

He kicks off dirt clad boots
leans back in chair
then smiles at her.

"It was a good day my love
thinking maybe, you'd be here
when I got home."

Sustenance

Oh, my darling,
I adore you so.
As sun to the flowers
you help me grow.

Water in your kisses
food from your heart
sustenance of soul,
you pour love into art.

As you humble me
teach me and dance,
my goal is to give you
more than romance,

but to water you also
with inspiration and love,
to treat you with honor
true as the sun shines above.

As a Wolf Breathes

for Eli Oliver Williams

Happy second birthday
lil man I've never met
Eli my nephew
son of brother whom I miss.
I was once two -tying tiny shoes
curious as today
more pure, less jaded less used,
but one thing I have learned
through many fierce trials,
that another day shall rise.
Perhaps on fire, perhaps rapacious
but it is always your choice
to be kind
to forgive others and yourself
to look within at how to apply
lessons from mistakes
to see how your actions, affect others
the humans the animals
the plants the oceans.
There is beauty in everything, seek it.
There is no light without darkness, be patient.
My brother and your mother
shall guide you with love
but one-day lil man it'll be your job
to pay this love forward
to practice your skills passionately
to fine tune your being consciously
to not let another, determine your will
to be Eli the Man strongest giant heart
walking intentionally, gently,

listening, seeking, boldly pursuing
what is right for your life.
Leave a wake of inspiration
for your successors.
Imprint goodness upon this world.
You are a rising King,
take your time,
be wise.
Instill love into everything.

With love, Uncle Wing.

A Walk Along the River

The sun crept further west.
We walked along the river, south
beneath firs, lodgepole pines,
ponderosa giants loomed highest above.
As the trail bent with the
raging northern force,
sun-slits 'tween wooden pillars
guided our steps,
illuminated turpentine ground ahead.
Words were exchanged
but so was silence bathed.

"I walk the trail and listen to the water.

Don't even have to see it.

I feel it."

Pen-Pals

As a child, school teachers
would give us a list of
other children far away
across the ocean.
Perhaps there would be
a picture attached
for all these children
would be ones I'd never met.
"Today you choose a pen pal"
she would say,
"for friends in other lands
help you grow in different ways."
So, one I chose and we relayed
maybe only 4 or 5 letters.
I did learn, of other kinds of breakfast
before similar kinds of classes
history of the world
told in different ways
literature
science
mathematics.
I learned that his parents
were not fond of Americans,
but he, just a boy,
wasn't sure why.

Premonition of You

Rowboat within rocked again
white cap waters -sane slashers -metronome
weights
swallowed vessel whole
d
o
w
n
into Poseidon's throat
disease of spins
leading to foolish whims
seeded sprout of eternal wisdom,
so, he stopped trying to drown.

The seas grew calmer
Eirene lifted his chin and bore
her dark brown eyes deep into portals of pain.
They made love beneath serene glassy water,
her petrichor skin wrapping
unraveled mystery of death
sifting earth-return into aqueous lungs.
She nibbled on shoulders toned
from lonely years long
licking scars of heart undone
she whispered songs
of another world that
replaced his swallowed dinghy
with a captain's ship.
She led him to Nirvana
and he never died again.

First Dance

Coffee brews with
excited patter tick
so drunk on caffeine
is hot glass pot
dancing the seizure
in its drip by drip
ebony brown
gathering spot.

I've rolled the
morning joint
no filter in it just green
so, when the dance
has ripened my dear,
we three shall convene.

River Release

"Why are you crying?" She asked.

"Cyclical nightmares of truth I wake up to,
weight of universal pain," he replied.
"I regurgitate into soil, which I am.
Then I stand again.
Why are you walking
out here with your eyes on fire
and your mind torn
to such worrisome pieces?"

She almost smiled as she turned
her canvased toe in dirt for some time.
With lip quivering she sat down upon the
muddy banks of river release,
between two worlds they wept,
ideas of pain bled into earth.

"Doors may not exist in this eternal hall."

"Nay, we just oft don't see them."

She slashed the air with finger nail colored.
"Is this a door?" She bemused,
which made him laugh
which made her fracture from the gray
and laugh too
and so him even more
and so she shrieked,
in howling variation

As a Wolf Breathes

as a train brakes and changes course,
rolling hiccups of laughter,
a push-me-pull of wheezy whats until
their tears had dried and only
raisin gasps of cleanse remained.

So, they both laid back to see
what shape the clouds were in.

"Yes, that is the greatest door,"
he finally replied.

Child Joy

A child
is amazed
by so much
like grown man
emptying
park trash
and recycle
into rolling cart
to bring
to bigger truck
to bring
to bigger dump.
As he putters away
little child claps
excited by
green spitting thing,
beam of sun
bright
upon her curious face.

Unencumbered

Aloft
between the ant and moon
where rocks
are islands separating winds
for eagles to slip out of drift,
talons grip a stubborn mortality.
Gargoyles lean precariously
pressing accomplishments
into pastes of past
mortar of rise,
catalyst to season's change
and perspectives evolution,
pinned upon
the silhouettes of horizon.
Matter of mine decay -evaporates,
emancipated from a fleshly prison,
lightness of an ethereal mind
now glides as the fly,
unencumbered by gravity.

Park Bird

You are black in flight
but as you boldly walk
on square stone cut for path
with head bobbing forth as
conveyer belt stuck, mechanically
attempting emancipation,
I see that you
are indeed only black in hew
but more -green blue purple even
guffawed silver when you puff
up like that to send shrill message
to foe, me, or lover.
Twelve feet you have scuttled
-perhaps more
giant S of many little steps
tiny talons making tiny noise
unlike
my shoes of wooden sole
old, like Holland.
Why do you walk bird
when you can fly?
Silly question -for I know why.
Same reason I suppose
of when I walk instead of drive,
simply to touch the ground
and move slowly,
intimately with the earth,
between the faster things.

Trey

'tis interesting
how some life happenings
hold amaranthine chords
that wrap around planet -gaseous dreams
soulful eternal arc
mostly minor 7ths or majors sustained
with muffled tonic peace
ghosts of tomorrow rest
with owls during sundial crawl
new moons shall not be feared
for knowledge awaits,

so
plant – nourish – harvest

like when we were thirteen and Trey was killed.
His last words to me
just before passage
shall always cantillate,
not in haunt
but in youthful wellspring,
comfort of beginnings that wear
more love than before.

"We do not know what the future holds,
my friend."

Bulldog Wrinkles

Pinot Noir
Chèvre crumbled
'pon warm French bread

garlic finger nail, onion sting pleasure

summer deluge arrives
with thunderhead eruption
as Louis' horn and he
cry tears
on cutting board
to drip
tacit flirtations
down
her umbrella –

after four bourbons, he lifts face to rain
she smiles slow
in black dress
red lips peaking
smoke slithering
scent of turpentine with sky weep
scent of skin on skin

carnal tangle until wax drips bulldog wrinkles

all shoes lay as passed out sloths
submitted to nonchalance
open window breezes kiss wet of exhaustion,
drink black coffee, smoke a cigarette.

Mother

The gondola was late.
Two minutes of torture
watching morning blossoms slowly float by,
fingertips of life
motherly drifts for babe swaddled in cloak.
She took them as a sign.
They would slip away in fading tendrils of night
before sun kissed the sky.
They would make it to the far shore.
Her babe would survive.
Lapping metronome of silence was disturbed
just slight,
she held him close 'gainst womb he had come.
Lioness eyes -sabers into night waning blue,
no breath to disturb this perhaps.
Visage glides closer
apparition of distance,
creeping demon she feared
demon she was prepared to kill.
Her right arm held babe close
hand over the ears of just beginning king.
Left fist wrapped revolver tight.
Slowly she raised the roscoe to address man
upon boat.
She exhaled slowly,
just a few more meters,
finger caresses trigger now warm,

just one more breath.

Unraveled

All the lil vampires now hang
upside down,
content furry faces
hum to dawn's feathery song
as I put the coffee on
as I prepare first smoke to send
signals to sun.
Blaring visage exponentiates
my third eye,
climbing far above
mountains -day old cupcakes
condensing,
evaporating,
preparing,
grumbling 'til dreams
harbored in blue long sleep
can breathe.
The smoke,
the coffee steam,
mountain breath,
soul once weighted released
from shackles of gravity,
we rise with the sun
into cosmic voyage
above the bats now asleep.

Ethereal song of the day,
mists of sleepy matter
unraveled.

Silhouettes

Mary Poppins held my hand in hers
then led me through florid door into
cornucopia of color,
avec un coup de rouge -Renoir land-
an ambling water
lapping toes afternoon
singing songs of riverbank
humming laugher into tunes,
shimmering eyes crossing
blossomed earth tones
sprinkled lavender glitter into hellos
with passerby's, with each other.
Freeze then dance,
paint then glance
at our glowing faces
cast upon the sun.
Petrichor children
holding colored pencils, we are, at
The Elephant Ear Drip Dreamland Bazaar.

Transformation

he looked
at her paintings
one by one

saturated by
her strokes
he evaporated

into an essence
beyond
wistful dreams

Transition

Smoke and steam of
tobacco coffee dance rise
in empyrean determination
morphing mushroom vine phantom
battled askew by morning rain,
Perhaps not an impedance
but grand gala of hoorahs
to each liquid descender
on sustenance plummet
to aeriform acrobats
wearing atomic messages
whisping wishes of universal roles
'pon tangle of interchange
from one league to another.
As the dragon and java breathes
mother milk descends my forehead.

Lovers Ensconced

They arrived a ravenous mess bringing the blizzard in with them. Icicles in beard, snowflakes on eyelashes, their hairs twisted together, his long in her earrings she made by the fire of lodgepole pine they both had harvested last autumn between making love in yellow aspen lounge by gold mine where his father had first taken him, where she first kissed him when they hid from the governments men ready and armed with steel spit and zeal, death if it came to that but today is not the day to die. They laughed like hyenas, earthen drapes spotted by winter as they untangled each other from carnal cave kisses, in auto blizzard capsule, necking before dinner and drinks. She held his hand, he brushed snow off her brown hair. "Two whiskeys two beers," they said in unison to barkeep Susan who lived out back in cabin older than them all three put together, she owned the joint. Susan smiled and shook her head, at their sloppy happy love, at the fun to come. The lovers sidled up to the long empty wooden bar for a raucous evening -of almost home.

Susan finished wiping clean the knife she held in her hand, dropped the bar cloth onto the floor, dragging it with one foot as she walked from hello to beer tap; the blood only remained by kitchen door now, lovers too ensconced to notice Susan's icy grin.

"Is Henry in tonight? He makes my favorite piccata." Lady lover of now unfrozen curls purred over her first beer sip.

"I'm afraid not my dear," Susan leaned over the bar as if to disclose a secret. "Just me tonight, but I promise you, my meat pie is to die for."

Bear Don't Care

Bear don't care if you are drunk
he will eat you anyway.
It is the hot sauce on chin
that sloppily dripped
before succumbing to the
slumber 15 beers in
that he may start with.
Laying sprawled by the fire
that has too gone to sleep
just a sparkle of embers
illuminating first sniffs at the feet
ground gently tremors
as man breathes slow
without knowledge of now
and how this will go,
stank of alcohol
to morphine the show
drunk grin
tasty warmth within.

Bear don't care if you are drunk,
he's gonna eat you anyways.

Positive Intention

Positivity inspires positivity.
As its opposite degrades such wellspring.
I have near dried out to death before
from drinking too long
the venom of negativity,
sitting in a garden of garlic,
strawberries, sweet peas,
I chose to feast on dust and thorns;
no more.
A warrior of goodness for myself,
for my relationships,
for this earth, I shall be -this I am,
yet as the strawberry is green,
and shall crescendo into red,
I am but the shoot first breaking soils ceiling.
The sun is warm on my face.
Conversations of healthy intentions
righteously warm on my heart.
The action of doing – embracing being –
pursuing betterment composes
star-count colors of joy within;
amidst the darkness
focus on the light.
Fight for goodness.
Infect negativity with intentional love.
Goodness will grow.

Omens

There are many messages impalpable
unless we honestly listen.
Omens are opportunities,
doors to enlightenment beyond
tangible learned apprehension.
To be deaf to such ethereal knowledge
is not what I choose.
I seek fruit for our future, not death.
When the world speaks it does so honestly.
The earth does not misguide,
it is what we choose to derive
for our own self gain that incurs wrath.
How ironic, to live for oneself
against universal grain only to kill then die;
this self-gain in the name of 'me first'
is not success despite temporary 'lordship.'
If you kill the plant you kill yourself,
for seed does not flourish
in a land stripped of sustenance.
As the storm approaches so tell the signs.
Observe the water, the wind, the birds.
Listen to the mourn of terns 'pon morning
zephyrs.
Humans did not invent the wheel
we were born into it,
let us not destroy it.

Icovellanva

Woke up a swashbuckler
sauntering forth then back atop hi-hat brass.

Toe-tips swishing blue linen sheet
other foot swaying free in troposphere.

Is it a victory swag to nightmare defeat?
Or is it fan oscillating lover's carnelian steam

that emboldens atomic tones
to orchestrate Medeskian beats?

Ah ho, I'll slow no show
of this pigeon bobble to sunrise notes.

I'll lean in even more with each bass slap
shimmering Aspen's morning amour.

Ra ta ta tahh, rah ye yehaww!
Rise with the sun of mountain thaw.

Bee de de YiYi! Dah Ri rah!
I'll tangle the sidewalks into icovellanva streets,

effervescent fusion astir in
mine empyrean aspiring feet.

Midnight Visitor

The gentle patter
from ocean tear's drift
reminds me
with turpentine scent
of that dark green droopy night
in Maine.
Between loon's 'hulaaa whoos'
a bear approached
my log lean cigarette smoke.
He looked down upon me through
sky drip sizzle
sniffing like a dog.
Drool fell slower than the rain
musk night-scape matted
in ebony steam,
paw claw shuffle sniff
considering my earthen posture,
so, I exhaled and said "care to sit?"
But, he just snorted on my fire
and sauntered off into the darkness.

Ranger Gray

"As I check one item off my bucket list, like drinkin' these beers here now at Phantom Ranch, well shit! I always end up adding a whole bunch more adventures to my list!" Ranger Gray leaned back upon cooler sand in canyon morning shade, his vein popping legs wearing that acquired extra layer of skin, dirt. "You really carried a damn 6-pack to the bottom of this hole eh, are you mad?"

I laughed for I was mad, madly in love with life and my life-sculpting ways. "Of course, Ranger Gray, beers down here, carried in by mule, after a big truck drives 'em all the way to Grand Canyon Rim, well damn they are so expensive! Plus, don't they taste better when you work for them?"

Gray rolled two cigarettes, handed me one, sneezed, blew his nose in a faded ripped red bandana, he waved it in the air as my smoke ascended the Anasazi hall. "This here was my son's, he died though," Gray disclosed matter-of-factly, he snot into the bandana again, chugged the second half of his second beer, so I handed him a third.

"Sorry Gray," speaking foolishly, fumbling for words, empathy, in the dry faded sand grit worn world we sat.

"Naw naw," he interrupted my dark room feel about. "Naw Wing, he gave me the greatest gift."

We both sat straight now, cross legged in scorpion path, looking the other into his eyes, we both brown, we both smoking, natives of the earth. "what was that Gray?"

"He gave me life."

"Yes, and so you gave him."

Gray smoked silently before he spoke, looking through me into the eternal beyond. "Ah but Wing, he taught me how to live. Sam was fearless, as I sat and obeyed my life away, he lived." Ranger Gray, shook sand out of silver hair, silver smoke curled higher, up, onward, "and so now Wing. I live for us both."

Wylie Verse

To spend night away from my dog
the reason must be so grand
that even in her palpitating heart
of jealous love, my shadow chasing
stealth-slinker understands.
She jumps into my arms,
forgives moon-long absence
only after skin of forearms
hands and face are tasted.
"Where ya been? Why the goofy grin?
It's not just food I want
It's to always roll wit you
my weird humanoid friend.
I got a bowl full of grain free,
got 'bout 39 toys
mostly ripped to shreds
cuz they gifts from you boy.
Murder death kill
I defend for I love,
barkin at birds loomin
too close above.
Soothsayers? Maybe.
Sky skatin crazies
swoopin awful low
to that I love most.
Best remind them
I'm the wild Wylie Wizzle.
I've a nose cold as cool
from digging earth tunnels.
I've tiger eye circles

As a Wolf Breathes

wrapping black hole funnels
that pull you, mesmerize you
drag you into soul tied universe
of where next to,
ride 'til we die
W. W. W. W.
You my inner mountain alien
and I'm yours too
you my two-legged freak,
I'm yo ebony Sheika
you my blizzard father
I'm your Colorado daughter,
so go on and leave
you'll return soon.
I'll be sleepin one eye open
while you lovers howl at the moon.
In unconditional love
I'll be pacing wolf den
always waiting my friend
to welcome you home again."

Morning After

Wine bottles lay empty
without ships
without waves to drift.
Soulless carcasses strewn
by cold fire pit
whisper soft as ribbon wind
slithers through trampled grass
whisping cork-less cavern lips.

Imbibed apparitions swirl
in purgatory brain
in artful effort
of tired cigarettes.
Pick the litter off the earth,
scrape
stand
rearrange.

Mystic island tolls bell of birth
singing starlight joys
yielding sundrenched pain.

Awakening

Radiant emissions
emancipated
from frozen desires
shatter darkness
like fireflies.
Heart thaw mists rise
with glittering
diamond auroras,
as heart
of marble scar
palpitates again.
Three-hundred
and forty-seven years
of grueling sadness
since cosmic soul embodied
ethereal celebration last.
So, with petrified breath
inverted to life
eidolon anima breathes
satiated,
until
sun and moon
wane again.

July

Ah the primordial drift
into an adolescent summer.

Sap shifters shed honeymoon gala
trading verdurous scarfs

for tawny weaves.
Tangle of languid humble greens

tinseled by sun warmth
before lovers open eyes

before coffee pot breathes,
barometers flux,

twilight skin emancipates dew drops
condensed from lip-slipped dream-words

vaporous brain dances
metamorphosing into salt beads

of morning caress.

Sage blues yawn as bear sloths dig.

Juniper gnarls wear medicinal sprigs.

Ponderosa pillars groan in alligator skin.

Wolf pants in velvet shade, as summer crawls in.

Perhaps

Constancy drips

as pendulum sings

as wine glass finger tempts

ribbon rainbows,

enlightened spectrums,

for mortal immortals

siphoning blood skins

into insatiable throats

as death woes

catalyze knowledge

to produce life and fruit

untarnished to consummation,

perhaps.

Apple Pie

I buy a piece of apple pie
with crumb crust,
no lattice like my love
makes out of threes,
but heavy soil tundra toppings
of cinnamon and brown sugar
earthen skin of molten goodness.
This piece is placed with care
within its museum quality casing
into itty corner of fridge that
tacitly has become 'food of mine.'
Oh, in the morning I shall eat you!
Slowly, with coffee and poetry!
No alcohol tonight after
evening run sweating out all
toxic existence within
body and brain. Clear
I shall be sitting in returned rays
illuminating morning bugs and birds
awoken just an hour before me.
A craving for this pie brewing
for weeks, from lover talks and
distant poet foggy train track
thoughts, relayed across sea.
Goodnight summer, goodnight lover
I whisper nestling in to
wolf run dreams, drifting into the fog.
Awoken by snowy mountain chase
I sit upright in rouge envelope
hand searching other-half

As a Wolf Breathes

for her warm skin, not today.
Dog stretches at foot of bed,
eastern giraffe drape allows
orange fluorescence to filter
into dream fog evaporation.
And so, after first bare chested
feet untested morning toke,
I remember, the apple pie!
The hunger leg-long-expunge
releases adrenaline grumbling
earthquake from innermost cave.
Up I jump and prepare ceremoniously.
First, let dog out, food for her
bounding grace, coffee pot on,
set of pushups, arrange lawn table
to face sun more, coffee pour
then to the electric cool box
to claim apple-icious luxurious
long awaited sustenance!

The refrigerator looks the same
as in the just dark night,
cool clean wisps of fresh kiss
my forehead and excited brown eyes,
but for one major detail.

My apple pie -is gone.
My apple pie is gone.

The apple pie was never mine.

Sometimes,

the pen feels so heavy
and fingers too stubborn to type,
but my brain will not slow
from its light breaking speed,
tornados slicing through another
pummeling sonorous angst
against mountain cliffs.

Like an imprisoned ibex
slaying nightmares awake
tiring only to ponder sanity
then walk calmly to water again.

She-Hawk's Flight

She soars
across the canyon.
Gentle glide
through aerial ribbons
as breath drawn
from soul, slowly,
on string
up belly and throat
out of mouth
into spaces adrift
into paint smudge
never dry-
to coalesce pastel's
peaceful pilgrimage
into
the all encompassing
light of darkness.

Hershey's Chocolate

The rapping of cages has begun.
Wooden scepter of jungle keeper
wakes the boys before the sun.
Makihl rubs broken thumb, reset
himself after evening beating
after barn door shut impeding
breeze that would have drifted
stench of piss bucket away
from sleeping cell. Curled 'pon dirt
as he did in the womb air's wet
cloak presses broken body.
Master was his mother now,
womb of tomb his freedom future.
There would be no work today,
Not until wounds tired to scabs,
until he could stand again.
Laceration vacation is what Olley
called days off as these,
Whilst rolling a piece of rice
slowly with his toe,
hands unable to grasp,
unable to work the cocoa fields.
Olley looked into Makihl's
deep black eyes, open graves
to underworld depths, demonic
staircases bleeding human breaths.
Tears bathed the two boys
as others stretched swollen limbs
and ebony scarred backs
standing to clang of metal bar bangs.

As a Wolf Breathes

Into the dawn single-file they trudged
leaving Olley and Makihl
alone in the cage.

Across the ocean
child in superman t-shirt
throws a tantrum in the park.
His mother reaches into purse and pulls
out a Hershey's chocolate bar.
Biting into Makihl's brown flesh
he stops screaming and laughs.
Biting into Olley's beaten flesh
he throws candy wrapper to the ground.
In a breeze it floats away slowly,
to dance in the wind
of American callousness.

Anima Rest

And lo,
the gentle waves
between
rise of heartbeat
'til rise again.
Peaceful lull of indifference,
lullaby of porch chair
rocking dreams
that saunter away
from glitter-winds diminished,
pixies nestled to bed.
Sun, moon and tide,
parity purity.
To roar the conch shell
when next wind arouses emprise,
a drift down
halcyonic river,
zenic eyes tender
to heavenly holes
scattered 'bove mountainous aspire,
to hymns of anima rest.

Path to Peace

As the town brims,
as others pour in
to dance and drink
'tween brick walls
'til sweat dries
leaving salt lines
on cottons and
trash strewn irreverent,
I seek the road
traveled by my
younger youth,
to bathe in consecrated
forests of reverence.

In the Forest

Where generations of turpentined decay
cracks ever so slight,
earth lips chapped
sprout gentle shadow flowers
timid to strangers.
Where mosquitoes waft
in vicious clouds,
stalking blood walkers who threaten
lake's (timeless?) rock caress.
Here, in sundial of twilight light cast,
I sit.
Orange lasts dissolve into aqueous
depths 'til bold return,
when woodpecker drums
in morning bore,
shattering
moss draped silence.

Lover's Lethargy

Tambourine herds
flood chalk doodled
sidewalk singing
sharp summer cheers
from riverbank to else.
Fifty brown paper bags
clutched with sandwiches,
maybe lollipops, bop
two feet off the ground
below window open
sifting shade's cool
western breaths.
Galloping gaggle
contained by adult
children wranglers
wake carnelian tangle
from unfinished slumber.
They anger not, as
eyes return to slips,
dream warmth from
verbal caverns are fused,
gently. Lullaby of
roving retirees,
mountain-bound
city escapees
and Tuesday 'must-be-dones'
blend together into
industry of beehive, tomorrow.
Beneath sheets - skin – pillows – leaves,
lovers sleep a little longer.

Odd Awakenings

What underworld
was I in?
That it
be so dark
I cannot remember,
only taste musk of terror
clinging behind eyelids.

As I wake
with portals open
to you again,

it is from death I return.

Candy Nightmare

I awake from a torrid dream. Safe in dark room, snug between her and window open with autumn's night breath near, the sun just a click away from its equatorial alignment, ash mounds upon intangible floor now spill out of eyelids and ears into the sheets warmed by two breathing beings. The curl of her relaxed fingers grasps my body in reaction to the scene my brain is ripped from; seething body in her tangle. My eyes fixate upon the fluttering leaves expiring upon nimble wooden fingers just beyond the no glass, my muscles soften beneath her sleeping sooth, mind returns to the vision before.

In this dream, along busy roads crossing each other this way and that, stores of convenience, markets of 'sustenance,' bazaars of children's blood, are filled with packages gleaming orange and blue, yellow, brown, red and purple. Bold blasting colors yell at consumers who listen, nay obey. Into the largest market I walk, candy coats all walls, Hershey's and Reece's and Snickers, Butterfingers, Mars Bars and Dove, sweets with notes of encouragement or Rumi inspired quotes within wrappers that say nice little things to the brains washed by monsters monopolizing each holiday, season change or occasion. The isles are longer than mine eyes could see down, each laden with colors containing souls from the bodies of sons and daughters sold, torn, deceived into slavery for the kings of chocolate to sit higher and higher on self-erected monoliths far above the sound of mourning.

Each isle filled with families wearing decent clothes, children holding hands, kind pleasantries being exchanged, no mayhem nor bickering, just endlessness emboldened by colorfully packaged toils. Gently, each human places parcels of orange and brown into baskets and stroll along in earth toned threads, red and black flannels for flatter. When children reach from perch upon carts towards the colors, each adult complies 'til no more candy could fit into any more baskets or carts. And so, long lines formed at the cashier booths. Cheerful patient queues snaking through the isles all of sway and smile, listening not to what they do not know, the quiet seep of ash.

From beneath each cart and basket, beneath each laughing body chatting casually with others in line, upon the floor which hold the consumers, amidst the dangling legs of children and shifting weight of teenagers, beneath the weight of adults with plastic cards that encourage, piles of ash build up as termite mounds with Babel-like dreams, rising higher and higher whilst sifting downward like the soot sliding flanks of volcanos. No one seemed to notice the rising putridity piling about their feet. The ash seeping as sand slowly from the corners and crevasses of each bag of candy colorfully packaged, covering the ground with the grey gone of lives seen not by greedy hordes of America. And if seen, then forgotten, or ignored, brushed away, who even really cares.

I screamed in horror, I begged the consumers to not purchase from companies who perpetrate and support the slave industry. Demonic greed breathing life into evil. NO! Do not buy from the hand that kills, choose fair trade instead. The ash had risen to levels above my mouth pouring down my throat suffocating all voice. And yet no one saw what was going on, they paid for the continuance of slavery and left the store smiling and laughing to prepare for another delightful American holiday. To spread cheer with neighbors and drink to the exuberance of ignorance. As they left others occupied their places, filling carts and baskets, handing over hard-earned dollars to scatter ash upon the floor and kick it into corners. Pattern of enslaver's footsteps upon the earth.

Awe

As a million green faces chatter
the comet's afterthought,
as tinsel beams flirt
on wind's diaphanous fingers,
prayers heard and dismissed flutter
down to dancing sand stones
welcoming wildebeest hooves,
dizzy diamonds in sun soak
silently seeking silver veil of
ballerina raindrop twirls,
second and fourths
palpitating to climax
when tonic stands drenched.
As shiver of anima starts with the toes
the carnal glitter crescendos
'til lips bleed soul-secretions
through earthquake breathes.
Mortal bodies reborn into butterflies,
draconian myths strewn cadaverous.
As mysteries empower clairvoyance,
as fractals evolve into jazz,
as élan-vital claws at the universe
scarring skies into stars,
I, and the world, tremble.

Until it Hurts

laugh us
to an orgasmic place
beneath the trees
where
bodies ache
from coursing endorphins
welcome daggers
slicing open
nectarine silliness
oozing out of brain
into eyeballs so wet
we now laugh
underwater

In Love

To be kind, as breezes
kiss sweat beads of heated exhaustion.
To be kind in love,
as wood stove glow on winter morning.

To be patient, as mother
with raucous cubs growing first teeth.
To be patient in love,
as a bodhisattva seeks nirvana.

To not envy, as the short
sunflower in back row of garden.
To not envy in love,
let joy flow, exalt the other's blessings.

To not boast, as hermit
with firewood and food box full.
To not boast in love,
as a silent knight defends the queen.

To not be proud, unlike tyrants
whom disregard righteous council.
To not be proud in love,
instead humble oneself to gentle accord.

To honor the other, as wind
uplifts a child's first kite.
To honor the other in love,
never to slander, always to protect.

As a Wolf Breathes

To not seek for oneself, meals shared
are medicine not only sustenance.
To not seek for oneself in love,
but gather wisdom, resources, gems, for them.

To not be angered easily, as a patient
owl awaits mid-summer nights.
To not be easily angered in love,
for gentleness and kindness, our practice.

To hold no record of wrongs, as mercy
and grace are the fabric of justice.
To hold no record of wrong in love,
but always forgive, always forgive.

Through any darkness persevere.
Trust the one you love
as a stone trusts time.
With each heartbeat exercise steadfast selfless
love.

Today

We are wrapped
in venomous vipers
decisions tangled by tubes
coursing imprisonment.
The fence beyond the
asphalt field wears barbed wire,
friendly reminder of
plebeian sheep patterns.
Metal rises from the ground
replacing life cut down,
dead bugs lay beneath
Edision ideas, blown to
cracks with cigarette butts.
Steal the water,
bottle the water,
sell it to the ones you poison.
Enslave the child,
beat the child
fill the mouths of oblivious
with chocolate blood.
Cancer sells cheaper than clean
so keep the masses diseased
and garner the proletariat's money
in your royal infirmaries.
"Tis just how it is,
what choice have we got?"
Says each
walking dead murderer.

For Safari

Flowin with the go,
thru owl wise trees
along goat spotted ridges
where sky sabers strike.
Nimble upon holy precipices
'til peregrine dives shatter
draconian expectations.
Cross gray asphalt snake
or let thumb drop traveling-feet
into another whoosh
of beer pints,
billiard hustles,
heart-beat boogies,
smokes lit as feet kick all doors down;
tho only for a moment.
To challenge the world with truth
W.C.W.K. must travel onward
breathing the sun and moons.
Baptism of brotherhood eclipse
forged in the land of aspire
inspires soul to lifelong ascension.
Sing and dance over fire and dirt;
share epic accounts of dragons tamed,
then nourish the wildernesses
of free will again;

for mountains are not climbed
by watching time glow.

All Passionate

Hedges grown full, wiry and untamed as
hair in the morning, reach beyond white
bars of wooden yard front, poor prisoners
contained for 'congenialities' sake.
Fingers graze each reaching sun seeker
tenderly, never to trim the quills of
Samson's summer, let natural cycles
breathe. The local street breeze rolls
through on popsicle tunes. Thank you
wind powered locomotive of comfort that
carries smoke of fresh lit cigarette east to
cross louder train tracks then ascend
beyond golden eagle road of high desert.
The act of cutting back, on cigarettes not
hedges, is considered. Across the street
tamer of green Einstein sweats, neighbor
under toiled forehead nods hello whilst
vigorously slashing to keep hedges
shaped like boxes. This, and the man yelling
his drug deprived demons at the asphalt
gift an odd smile. How different we all
are, and yet – all passionate.

INTO THE ZEPHYR
DOWN TO THE RIVER
TO DIVE WITH THE OSPREYS, I SAUNTER.

For a Friend

You are the anchor now,
lonely island drifter
floating
to cloudy top of
heart saturated oceans.
Generation's crescendo
of wisdom tears drip from
dreams into neck perspiration
kissing skin tenderly
as if it were still a babe's.
For we all are petrichor children
nestled in the bosom of mother.
We all unfettered anchors
floating silently in time's turn
'til the duty of aeon ripens,
to stand as she did,
eternally cloaked
by the ethereal stellar strength
of mother's love.

Comfort from a Tree

I sat on the edge of the cold damp field wanting to die. The river before me which once bred joy and love now beckoned my end. My heavy weighted end. I considered moving my toes first, but that was too much. To move anything now would require strength I did not have, no power of brain, no passion in heart, too comfortable in dark hole creeping up around legs and waist and chest and face hoping this would suffocate me, end me without having to even move. Let me die. I could see the devil smiling, I could feel his hot breath on my heart, I closed my eyes and melted into sadness and anger.

The ground began to rumble, gently at first. My back which sank into the trunk of a giant oak now scratched at my skin as the ground shook the tree's core and giant limbs flailed above in fury. I looked up to the giant as his green leaves fell upon my face. He was not angry as I first imagined, he was dancing. He was smiling. His arms waved back and forth pouring confetti upon this cold, damp field.

I jumped out of my chasm and faced him straight on. "Let me be! Why must you dance when I want to die. When I am dying. Must you mock my pain? You ugly horrid tree!" I held my fist up to the beast as he bowed lower to see my angered eyes, so close I could smell sweet sap dripping from his gentle giant wooden tree mouth.

He breathed into my pores. "This is no place to die friend. But only to live."

"Leave me." I quickly retorted in return. "I am not your friend, you do not know me. "

"Ah, but that is where you are wrong, I do know you, and where am I to go young unsettled soul? I am a tree."

I walked paces forth then paces back trying to drain the angst, sadness, fury within out like change through pockets with holes to the ground.

"How so?" I responded with less hate.

"Last summer you slept beneath my shade seventeen times. You and your friends would hang sweat stained clothes upon my fingers as you swam and laughed and danced. You smoked more marijuana under my arms than any other company I've hosted."

I laughed short, but I did laugh and the giant tree smiled and laughed in return clearly encouraged by my quick smile.

"Yes, yes you did, I would see you coming from miles away and know oh boy, to the stars!"

"Hey!" I quickly interjected, the tree seemed to be getting a bit too excited. "That's my line."

"Oh, I know my friend. To the stars."

"Go get yours," I spoke back smiling now, forgetting the immediate pangs of heart wretched pain. The tree bellowed with deep rich laughter, leaves once again decorating the now clear blue sky with green shimmers kissing now warm sunlight as he roared.

"Go get yours, another of your choice phrases, this too I know." He smiled.

"Aye." I spoke and looked at this giant tree with new eyes, I smiled.

"You were always there for me, even as of now huh."

"Yes, my friend," he bent close once more and spoke deeply with the genuine tree voice I didn't know I so needed. "You will hurt more, you will feel all alone, but this is not the place to lose your mind. You must pick up that crazy heart, (a gentle wooden finger pointed at my chest) you must journey on and up. There is greater. You must my friend, you must." His eyes oozed sincerity, sap teared down his trunk, he breathed so deeply, almost choking on his last words. "You must my friend." His trunk resumed its tall wide stance. His eyes closed. I looked at him with forgotten love. Aye, I must.

As a Wolf Breathes

I walked up to the river and crossed it jumping upon choice rocks embedded between highways of healthy trout. A river of life I noticed again. On the opposite bank I looked back at my tall gnarled oak tree, then forward and up to the mountain in the distance. 'He speaks wise words but I fear he does not know how black my soul is. But for him I shall try once more.' My eyes locked upon the greatest mountain far beyond. I must climb it.

Sharpening Pencils

Nights
        not be so grand
as spinning through shooting stars atop hills,
honeypot breaths stirred
        falling
               into laughter and sweet grass.

Days
        need not concoct adventures
that summon each adrenaline magician
to brim of sky fly aspirations
        within
              our flavor seeking souls;

though this we do naturally,

though discovering new valleys
of marvel and night-nooks of love
become diamonds within our mosaic,

there is just as much magic
              in the plain.

For the true glitter darling,
        is simply being next to you,
even
        if we are just sharpening pencils.

Petrichor Orchestra

After the rain has ended
and wind arrived at
today's destination,
after bird bathes
rippled lake tops
wine glasses on picnics
livestock troughs all
cease aqueous dance,
puddles remain
filling earthen pores.

Mirrors to hat rims,
thirsty chipmunk eyeballs
bottom of kissing chins
up-skirt reflections
finger's casual sway
glimmer – with each light touch.

Tree breaths are now
almost seen as
all is mist and tangible
coalesced, petrichor
orchestra of scents
in shaken hydro-bubble
shooting across the cosmos
holding slight to the sun.

As a Snail Moves

'Twould be a hot day
sunrise indicated,
the air already a tired flavor.
Horizontal Z's tangled
skin suction cupped,
lethargy of bedroom sauna
with sheets on the floor.
Mini dragons buzz in
through window
we hung out of
to catch the 2am breeze,
smoke agents of love cast
to sturgeon's waxing moon.
Dog already pants
though she hasn't moved,
guitar in corner has swollen,
b-string has broken.
Jazz stirred to inspire vertical rebirth
succeeds slowly,
for lips taste of salt, dreams and desire.

Grit

Another no entry clause.
Doors open doors close.
Seems to be too unclean for me
is what they eventually decide.
Singaporean fashions seeping
into frontier bloods tamed,
ahh 'tis a damn shame.
So many of them.
All I am is me.
True health lies in balance
there is no life without ash.

You clean the glass,
I'll be the grit.

Painters of Possibility

Whisk me away
on a summer night adventure
full of nooks where owls
tell tales that we
scribe into books made of
willow bark on the bank
of a river.
Sashay atop the water we will
'til tender dimensions
swallow our skin and each
garment is surrendered
to hand coddling darkness
and swan like behavior.
The stars observe as we
ride wild mustang shadows
from alcoves to ledges,
our dyadic lupine howls
the sustenance of wind.
Composers of magic carpets
we are, on epics adrift together,
Painters of Possibility on
a summer night adventure.

Supper Preparation

Horses graze with slit eyes
Arabian tails swish about flies

irked not, for the evening
is nothing but a blade of grass to chew on.

Incandescent heart glow,
potato peels, crystal rainbows scatter porch

teeth wear jalapeno seeds
boots aside toes breathe,

gaze dedicated west
where she shall soon slice the setting sun,

her visage a graceful silhouette
of gargantuan soul warmth.

Her hands the bearer
of wild herbs and flowers.

Feline Adaptation

The great flash bites again.
        Saber of sky regurgitated,
        blanket of cover interrupted
        all silence – shattered,
        as he drinks from spring
        at head of earthen crevasse.

Pupils constrict sharply,
        orbs of confusion remain
        (brain-flies pulsing in
        now darker darkness)
        scent of grasses smoldered
        to torrents thirsty rip
        encompass air-tell drifts,

glow of eternal roll
        pillages progress of stealth
        though terror will lead
        deer to death.

Iron jaws are patient.
        Crackle of ponderosa pillars
        groan to hellish disintegrations
        which he circumnavigates
        quietly upon pads of practice.

Orange eyes await,
        shadow catchers
        no soot coated refugee
        could escape.

Find Joy in the Pilgrimage

Covert cavalry
-was how he put it
with a smile, I did not believe-

bathing in bosoms of only harvest.

Whether it works for him, I doubt,
some balance, some fall into depths,

whoremongers of misunderstanding
litter the earth,
-they not the sun,
simply, at odds with themselves-

apathetic of empathy,
-he lied,
upon asking why black coffee
suited me better than sweet.

"Cream exists only in my destinations
never my journey," I reply,

to which he leans back
as I tighten battered bootlaces.

The Waltz

Confined by swaddling cloths
tighter
and tighter,
helplessly rolled
darkness' crepe to nibble upon,

demon caterpillars eat my skin
python burlap sacks envelope
fighting brain limbs,

never surrender
to moldy breath of monsters return.

I tear
I claw
I gasp for life

with fingernails imprisoned
beneath weights so great
they fall
into torn tatters of blood
as I am wrapped,
constricted,

brain beaten
-violently.

Prisons of Not Me

Switch off the headlights
and look clear with your brain,
eliminate the traps you've created
to stay safe,
excuses mounded generations tall
created simple sheep
infatuated with walls.
For your choices seem
elaborately invested
in material decay
and early impressions,
desperately fighting
to ward of witches
like myself alive with
independent decisions
from you,
from the tyrants you
comfortably cling to
I bare my teeth gleaming
sun-fractal proud rainbows
-my own way to be.
Decisions of others may
be your modem,
partisan to moth eaten golds
and slavery continuum,
for if sheep all get along
we will never have the problems
of lone wolf
kind thoughts,
kind decisions,

morality,
of challenge greater
than what they be.
You burn the gasoline
I'll smoke the cheef
walking happily away
from prisons of not me.

A Fresh Page

The clink of silverware above my head drifted its way through open balcony doors. Footsteps shuffled on pitter-pattering floors enticing me to turn and enter the promising remedy for my grumbling stomach and aching soul. A faded red paisley carpeted staircase led me upwards to the blond hostess. She sparkled, "Good evening sir, how many are with you tonight?"

Rustic floorboards remembering dance steps a century old stretched across a wide-open space. An old blues boy tuned his Les Paul guitar in the brick corner. Gold brass railings shone clean, her smile brought comfort. "I am alone, thank you, I will be happy at the bar."

She smiled sweetly and spoke kindly, "happy to have you, Eddie is playing tonight, you are in for a treat." I couldn't help but smile back warmly as I turned towards the old mahogany bar.

"Hows it be?" The bartender in a casual white slapped down a menu boppin' his head to a tune within.

"It be's good brotha. You have a house cab?" I responded with less bop, settling in and remembering the days before. This is what I needed, new energy. I was in the right place. Bartender Tony slunk a glass of red in front of me, I sipped it satisfied and grabbed the menu. Bustle grew around me as I slipped inside my mind, remembering the days before.

~ ~ ~

"Looks like we will be separating again then huh. Might not be seeing each other for a good bit." G spoke calmly as I paced and fumed. We stood alone in the woods, upon an exposed ridge between the pines, at high elevation in Northern California. He let me rip and spit as I dragged my smoke.

"I'm just exhausted man. I need to get my soul back. You must understand. I would love to hike 10 more miles with you tonight, but I don't know… This shouldn't be happening at this point, my motivation, my vigor has weakened. First the giardia, then my brother's wedding back east, in all that unexpected long time off I lost the powers amassed after hiking from Mexico. I am killing myself on miles when my body needs to slow down, just a bit, recoup, then I'll be back."

I spoke with a frosting of hope even though my heart had none, for my brother's sake, for Sam whom I'd known since the hot limping days of desert fatigue. My boy who'd grown right before my eyes from a restless dormant man to a confident motivated new soul. "I will always live a legendary life." I clamored waving my ice axe savagely around above my head drunk on cheap whiskey a few moons before. "So that is why I will be hiking up and over the summit of Mt. Whitney the hardest way I can with or without you."

Sam, G, my boy stood up opposite I, the fire bouncing off mountain boulders strewn. His voice stone with promise. "I would never let you go alone. I am coming with you." That is who he is. My back, my brother, a comrade in combat against the average or anything less than more. Another 'alpha' to co-lead greater ideals around the world. A higher bar.

"Here we are fellow hikers, fellow humans, let us not allow this path, this skinny destined path be our only focus. Our journey is far wider than that. To leave a world of draconian social restrictions and then come here in search of freedom only to bind ourselves into a new prison of only purist trail, path, this damn brown thing and that's it!? No, let it be more. It is what is around us, the accidents, diversions, the challenges, the pain, the people, unexpected gifts of generosity and human love. It is the idea that even this can be elevated if we let it. That confidence bred here should be used out there. That kindness received here should be given forward everywhere. Hike onward North to Canada yes, but take off the horse-blinders and stomp them into a fire for it is the more that makes this truly yours."

~ ~ ~

A red sauced fra diovolo with plenty of seafood glowed before me on the menu. The hostess whom had first greeted me stood beside dropping off half empty beer glasses forgotten at door by smokers distracted. I leaned in her direction gaining her dish review.

"If you do not like it I will eat it, spicy and creamy, they make it right."

"Then I suppose I should order for two." I joked as she smirked and ran off to greet new hungry arrivals. I settled in, thanked Tony as he refilled my glass heavy with red and returned to deep crevasses within my mind. Eddie began to play his guitar.

~ ~ ~

G charged forward, I lagged behind, letting distance between us grow until I could see him no more. Why is it that I crave friendship, company, comradery yet push everyone away? I awake wishing to be held safe in the soft arms of a beautiful woman, or that I can just yell a 'good morning' to a friend a camp away, and then every force in my body stops me, angered by the sight of another soul perhaps tortured too. Scared, ducking into undergrowth I hide from being seen. I dream of shared company on mountain summits and company to bath and splash with in alpine lakes, but then they may see me weak like this.

As a Wolf Breathes

I stopped alone on the ridge's edge feeling more confused and trapped than ever before, besides being shackled by another man choosing to control another, shackled now by brain. Before me lay endless miles of dark trees. Behind me lay endless miles of dark trees. My friend could only hear of this confused pain, but not see it, he mustn't. I will be alone for this purge, no one will watch my fight with the devil.

The sun hung above distant peaks promising more evening light yet I chose to not go on. My knees hit the rocky ground as I groaned. Why was I trapped, where had my motivated soul gone? Why did the line 'even the inspired can die' plague my grinding mind? What had happened? I did not want to go on. For what lay ahead? Was I walking into a black hole simply delaying financial stability, real relationship or an ultimate complete personal crumbling destruction, walking a slow death. What does it matter or even mean if I complete this pointless hike? The mountains will be here, my sanity felt far less so. This was not me. Incorrect this was me but I would not accept this confusion and misunderstood internal autochthonous torturous pain. Where is the strength I had acquired?

Breathing slowly, meditating upon the truth, I forced myself to begin a true mental readjustment. The ridge I sat upon dropped off steeply below my dangling feet into dark Northern California forest. The peaks beyond surely lay in Oregon. I was nearly to a new state, a fresh page. 1,700 hundred incredible miles of California lay behind me, they had blessed me, tested me and allowed a seed of discouragement to be planted of recent. The seed had grown and now festered my soul with invasive poison. It was time to cut the stalk, pull out the roots and be rid of this disease once and for all. I stood up and forced myself to continue hiking north one leaden step at a time.

~ ~ ~

My food arrived and Eddie began to play. I looked at myself in the giant bar mirrors standing behind an assortment of liquors and mixers. I smiled remembering I was now in Oregon. A fresh page. The sauce was good, the prawns better, and the air heavy with expression. I had made it, I was in Ashland. A beautiful town of love likening a multi-colored quilt. Transients filled the squares between the backpackers and the hippies. Marijuana was smoked openly and given freely. Beneath shaded trees on cool summer grass in parks harboring jugglers, lovers, mothers, and pups, I had rested. I had made it, I had motivated myself out of another black brain hole, away from my should be sanctuary, the deep dark forest that had haunted me just days before.

~ ~ ~

"Walk yourself well. Walk yourself well Wing. You have done this plenty of times before." I spoke to myself as night began to saturate the wilderness. "You must remember why you are here." A small could be flat campsite unveiled itself beneath a dark grove, the perfect place to be alone and let myself listen, think, forget, dissolve, remember.

The night wrapped itself around me as the forest became alive. Surrounded by bears, lions, wolves, fisher-cats, wolverines, fox, porcupines, snakes, owls and cool tender mountain breath, the trees began to sing a nighttime lullaby. This is the world I loved, the world in which I had learned to find peace within my soul amidst imperial depressions. This world is my home.

A flying squirrel zoomed by out of nowhere, landing upon the tree I sat beneath. Wand of wind breaking ethereal grains. An incredible zip of freestyle soaring. I laughed amazed as his black body peered out at my headlamp quickly clicked on. I bellowed out a loud long resounding KOOOIEEE sparked by the moment of peaceful woodland solidarity, kindling of inspiration had arrived. It shattered the darkness as a double edge sword of remembered joy. The distant responding KOOIEE of a comrade another ridge away inflated my vigor. Surely that must be Sam now miles ahead.

I beamed and danced in the darkness remembering I am not alone in this. I have a community, a family, a following of supporters whom I live for. This is not about just me. It has grown into rich velvety layers of purpose and community love, of relationships birthed creating a better world than when I began.

Each mile I hiked bred another genuine interaction. Blessings of love, knowledge and compassion had showered me. A nod on the street, admiration from day-hikers, a free sandwich because I walked, my grandmother's prayers, a kind ride to town and back, afternoons spent sharing extravagant stories. Beds, showers, food and drinks were all given selflessly by humans I had never before met. I'd been hugged, kissed, supported and inspired. My walk had given me more than I could ever dream so why would I stop now. I owe everyone that.

The confusing murky weight which had hindered my motivations afore now fell as decayed shrouds from my soul. I had remembered and become re-inspired. Get to Oregon, get to Ashland, talk to people, laugh and listen, write the way I must, and go share something real. This is why you walk, always pursuing the greater, so hold your head high and fight the good fight.

His Drift

See the bird
flying across the sky,
encumbered slight
yet confident,
on smoky draft
he somewhat meanders
like husband
with simple vices
headed home
to the woman he loves.

Poetry to the Sky

As she sleeps by my side
angelic curls, sonorous sighs,
risen sun slithers in
touching tangle of golden skins.
Closer within my nook
she nestles, tender warmth she wears,
fingers ne'er erring off
from grasp of me beneath sheets soft.
Her wrap I will not leave
'til she has satisfied her dreams;
careful not to move much
I grab a book, she tightens touch.
And as nest is arranged
to taste the drips of midnight rain,
she holds my heart as I,
whisper poetry to the sky.

We Must Evolve

Seething, it seems.
Phlegm of death sprinkled,
torrents of hatred inebriated
on siphoned songs of hell.
Wind carries emberous seeds
soul sins stained 'pon soil
from polar bears sunk
bone-bag's eyes last drip,
from enmity threatening love
ecocidic warfare unleashed,
human righteousness
supported by leaders unfit.
The bear shall bite the sun
in retaliation for what we've done,
the land shall perspire ash
until cessation of wicked acts.
This imbalance must be defeated
the earth and its inhabitants restored
nay, evolved beyond the constant
crumble of history's repeated falls.
For as noon glows blood imbrued
orange and gray, color of last days,
she, the all of ever was, weeps.
-this is not the way-
beneath moons waning eye
she shrieks and shutters violently,
shrouded sky tears disseminate amongst
the seekers of renewal,
upon educators of salvation,
upon the warriors opposing hatred,

As a Wolf Breathes

upon the children of flowers
who believe – we must evolve.

Your Breath

Your breath travels across my chest
as autumn sun whispers in the taiga

slipping through tangle of hair
gentle lasers of caress
wisp through trees
beyond cheek's repose

each in roll, as ocean berth after
tempest has dissipated to glass,

long strokes of a rowboat 'cross
a silent bay, if silence
was the murmur of birds and breeze
ne'er distracted from the sea,

as a zen master breathes
you respire gracefully,

asleep upon me.

Mental Escape

They kidnapped him for a mission
to which he disagreed
then set him upon a metal bench
in room of 100 degrees.
fan blowing hot air
direct upon his face
chained to melting incisions,
his saliva evaporated
til no more could he speak,
though eyes still smiled tenderly
at the thought of her painting
scenes of forest families free.
Here he would escape
his mind unchained
despite the spit of slander
dripping down his neck.
Mortician shook the hand of the guard,
they called each other by first names.
The concrete scrape of others before
who never wore agreement slithered
as rivers seen from outer space.
"A rudimentary adjustment
is all he needs.
Abecedarian recoding,
too entrenched in the verse of earth,
and worse – he may be in love."

They did not conceal their voices,
verbally unveiling opinions of control.
A long leash of teeth and tongues

As a Wolf Breathes

was dragged through the blood
beyond the door, into hellion's hall
where he sat awaiting perhaps death
-tho belief in morality still incurred hope.

They dropped the rope of voices silenced
at his feet. Through eyes swollen
beyond his barrage of zeal
he meditated in the darkness.

~ ~ ~

She tinseled the world
with radiant laughter.
She twirled in a summer dress
then landed upon his chest
to kiss the beat of aspire they shared.
Shining goddess of the moon
held his heart with her own
caressing the light beyond.

By Her Side

Shoes strewn askew
pinecones rearranged
to make room for carpet
of artful amour.

Silence bequeathed
kiss inhalations
'til guttural climax
of laughter's aspire.

On riverbank
by her loving side
all poems, paintings, songs
embolden my soul.

The Two Fishers

Each waded in water on opposite side of river
intent beneath the gurgle of rapid's ease to
amble.
The heron and the man never minded the other;
artful predators, ballet of baptismal evolution,
silent howl, primitive instincts, gems unearthed.

Juniper scent undulates with river mist rise
to greet my petrichorilian lean.
I and the trees breathe quietly in warm breeze
as the two fishers fixate below.

Blue like berries – if it was dusk,
bearded soothsayer gray
wisely thrusts white neck
(as mulling kings speak)
into intentional depths.
Each beak emersion glitters
not of adolescent pride
but as Ol Ironsides floats,
water drips from heron's swallow,
cast against setting rays,
flow of heart patience, persistence.

Human emulates the hunter's strike.
In time, perhaps a fish is hooked,
yet of this I do not know
for as Great Blue flies away
grandly fed, royally satisfied,
pendent upon heavenly vines

As a Wolf Breathes

-I do as well,
soaring through forests of peace;
Ponderosa & Juniper.

Shadow Lane

walking
down
the street
hopeful no one
comes by
swigging
an evening
lullaby

sunflower
sidewalks,
scarecrow
shadow
ahead
or is it
the animas
of long ago
dead

Overcome

-How much water can you hold?
Poseidon challenged him.
-More than you can mount.
he replied bluntly.
Silver horses galloped
from trident fingers
spewing rain upon visage,
tsunamis from
earthquake breaths funneled
down throat to
Mariana Trench depths.
Each drop of liquid
expanded his soul 'til
he floated away
upon cosmic drifts,

having become the world.

Cooler Wind

On cooler wind of shorter days
the haunt of autumn's dim wet grace
slips her fingers beneath the fringe
of tighter threads and heavier beds.

She seems to me to be the queen
of ethereal song in season's change,
winter whisperer at the door
crawling slow upon earth's floor.

Summer's slumber has surrendered,
sinews stretch as leaves slowly weep,
rising eruption of colorful drape
bows to weight of skeletal fates,

for lo the changing wind blows
o'er ocean growl n mountain groan
settling deep within the bones
'til a fire is lit and lovers moan.

Treasure Chest

A treasure chest
buried beneath centuries
I emphatically dig out,
sifting sand
once clay
slides volcanically
down dream slopes away
after another epoch's water
dared to veil secrets forever
-then rivers now canyons,
remnants of an old canoe,
rust of golden promises polished
until corrosion is abolished,

breathe life into potential,
tarnish no more.

Bloom

It took me many years of living, much pain, many
mistakes, awful actions and patterns, destructive
thinking and improper focus, misguided channels
of export self-imposed, imbalanced practices and
greedy egotistical blindness to symbiotic
existence within this universe,

until,

mine eye began to open,

a butterfly cocooned for so long,
an age of undetermined value,
an envy for those more mature than I
in younger bodies,
shedding the envy
is another step towards bloom,
as is mourning sins
and wasting no more time,

for now,
as the layers are peeled away,
as I am exfoliated of before
I beat and breathe for one reason,
to love as water feeds
to love as warmth wraps,
to fight for the power of kindness
and the treasure you all are.

Breakfast for Dinner

A purple sky at 7pm,
owl signals dark hours begin
honey retrieved from the cabinet
blankets wait as lover's fabric
kettle sounds the shining shrill
of healthy warmth within,
her waffles and whistles
sooth my heart,
her smile tears all anxiety apart,
breakfast for dinner is the way
we feed these steps of after-day,
for when the moon is past its noon
our howls shall tell of dark's end soon
and owl and we shall slide beneath
the golden curtains of night's reprieve.

October Wind

The wind is an Alice Cooper anthem,
a great rake with a great wake
siphoning forth hordes
of graduates and dropouts,
slurping souls of sap
to scatter as bovines stampeding
across everything,
down all streets over each car
into the faces of sunglasses and scarves,
the mighty song of Pied the Piper
is each emboldened whoosh
as red and gold and orange flocks
violently battle forth – to their death,
to their snow weight hibernations
to their eternal sustenance of life;
'one last show before we must go'
dancing on the limbs of alley tornados,
then piled in yards
or pinned to the collage
of a teenage girl with grand dreams
and an eye for essence.
Outside her window the wind
drags blue clouds across the twirling earth.
A great tree once standing green
now bows to season's change
with sacrificial humility.
"Take all of the wisdom I wear
then let me rest,"
the girl imagines the tree gently whispers,
so, she wraps herself in a shawl

As a Wolf Breathes

and walks out into the yard,
to be swaddled by the truth of time.

Practice Kindness

For though the rose may wither
as a hawk with no more feathers
in the melancholy winds that whisper omens,
autochthonous animas howling for repentance,

for though the earth trembles upon its
celestial tendrils
begging to be walked upon lighter,
to not be the home of a species of hate,
fatigued beneath a feet-fury tread of injustices
mourning for peace as blood drips deep
into her gullet drowning the very sobs she wails,

for though time turns a fresh coat of paint
into yesterday's barn wall,
mortal beneath feces of ants
and snake skins shed,

kindness is not paint, nor mortal.
There is much we must do.

Begin again.
Each day we choose,
that within my realm-reach of ripples
however far the wind
carries my word and action,
in every moment of synergy – I shall be kind.
I will not use my previous failures
to undermine my now,
I will not judge the soul of another

As a Wolf Breathes

with putrid impartiality,
I will not promote a culture
of harassment and abuse,
nay I shall fight it.
I will not turn my eye
to any darkness within,
to ego, to weakness,
I shall be strong,
I shall practice love.

If I fail let the chaff dissipate,
impurities released as nevermores,

then stand and begin again,
sharper
softer
emboldened.

With this practiced,
in this we shall grow,
as flowers baring our petrichor hearts to the sun,
rising amber song, a field undressed
of all hatred and wrong,
we, the unified warriors of love.

Dreamland

There is a wonderland which lays ahead
existing always without me,
dreamland beyond the curl of smoke,
blue hues of pure frost tenderly coating
the skin of everything
clean and crisp
bountiful in breath
free from constraint,
as birds whose wings are never injured,
uplifted wishes of wellness
return as sunbeams
caressing all as octopi love
wrapping each portal of pleasure
with sensual sustenance;
the evocative joy of discarding
all shackles of addiction
chained no longer.
Land of dreams you shall be destroyed
for I now claw through the fog
to bathe in the bosom of reality,
controlled by addiction no more.

Grateful

You may already know this,
wise aware woman,
but I shall tell you anyways.
Around you the whole world
vibrates brighter, ripples
of positivity, sunflower faces
uplifted, beats of inspiration
all emanate from
your graceful kindness.
and as we kiss,
this you may not know,
I am silently thanking you,
passionately telling you
with our pressed lips
of how grateful I am, for you.

The Cabin

The cabin laid asleep beneath the snow. No footsteps led to its barred entrance for no one had entered in many years. The door stood buried by cold drifts winter wind had created. Only the one window on cabin's western wall showed top of lonely eye, dark and cold in hibernation. He walked up to the window, dropped to his knee and dug out the bottom half then lay upon his belly to peer in. Elevated far above the frozen dirt beneath winter's blanket, a man would be buried standing up and that'd be the end of him, wrapped in freeze if his feet did touch the ground. Despite the time, despite the cold weight the window pane remained unbroken, within was the furniture he once built, within was the shovel he would need to dig out the door, and much more. He would break this window and crawl in, get a fire going to thaw out the cabin who slept here in wait for his return.

Stone smokestack breached the white pack heavy upon cabin-head though icicles reached to the ground, evolving stalactites creating unwelcome gate of frozen spears. Before breaking the pane, he walked around the entire cabin slowly, snowshoes keeping him afloat. All was well, the wood he split still sat beneath the overhang in the back, corner bits of green tarp stuck out of the ice, this too he must dig out. The wood will burn well, it had been three autumns since he fell the trees and split the pine, three cords of juniper too that would burn hot, this he must conserve; though with nearly fifteen cords of lodgepole pine he would survive the rest of winter.

Behind the cabin, fresh tracks of rabbit and bobcat dotted the snow, one behind the other. He walked deeper into the forest behind the cabin following the animal's trail for half-a-mile, it was slow moving which he cherished, looking up into the trees he had not seen for so long, trees he thought perhaps he would never see again. They led him to the aspen grove where he used to lay beneath the quivering gold, winter winds gray upon the horizon. Here he realized he had lost the mammals' tracks only to stumble upon some new, moose, they had been here recently. Surely enjoying the sweet bark of deciduous, perhaps bedding in willow thickets beyond the open meadow by frozen pond beyond the grove. He would explore again soon, but first he must warm his sanctuary and cook the dinner he still carried upon his back. Darkness would arrive within the hour.

As he turned back to the cabin a breeze rolled in. It carried sweet scent of juniper, lodgepole pine, ponderosa from further beyond mixed within the cold dry of wet. The greatest smell in the world he thought, as his stomach churned imagining the aroma onions, garlic and meat would bring tonight. No, though petrichor be a scent of his soul, the greatest would be that of her... Melancholy here was comfort, for in this wood beneath these giants of time sadness was allowed, this freedom bred joy. He smiled and picked up the pace back to the ol cavern asleep beneath the snow. Thinking of how pleased she would be to see these cold wise trees. He missed her hand in his, and so held his right hand as a fist, as if her fingers were within.

The window broke easily, nothing a swing of an ice axe couldn't muster. He knocked away the sharp chards that grinned at his endeavor, they fell into the musk that flowed staunchly out into the forest, up into his nose as he poked his head first within the fortress. 'Ah yes, a table beneath, I got this.' He dropped his pack and rolled around to lower his left leg slowly down 'til toe touched the wooden table top, careful not to rip his drawers, careful not to catch his coat on broken shards, he entered successfully. It felt as a fridge, the cold insulated and compounded here in this dark box. Looking back to the window, day's remaining light cast a soft glow, snow dropped down onto the table from outside. He pulled his pack through the hole, then his snowshoes. It was time to work.

Out of pack he pulled his headlamp, went ahead and set the bag of extra batteries upon the table, after the work outside was accomplished he must take inventory of all he had. The headlamp was a good one, beat and bruised but it shone bright. In the front right corner of the cabin he spotted three shovels where he had left them. Two big plastic scoops for snow, one hard metal shovel for dirt and ice. Dust covered them all, dust he had not seen since town mixed with the snow into slop that lined the roads; a deep long five miles walk below. He smiled at the dust, at the idea of time and the shovel's unknowledgeable patience. Into it he pressed his bare hand gently to look at his finger prints finely designed into the silt.

'Alright'.

With choice shovel in hand he unlatched the bolt holding shut the heavy wooden door, he pulled it to him, hard, the creak of ice unwilling to give, he smacked the sides and gave it a kick then pulled harder once more, into the cabin it opened pouring an avalanche of white and waning day light. To accomplish any task in life one must first take a step, here a first joust with a shovel. Once he had dug into the frozen world in front of his cabin he had broken a mighty sweat. He ripped off his jacket, head getting stuck within darkness but a half second till his sweater steamed. He took a long pull of water, too easy to get dehydrated up in the mountains, all the dry despite all the wet.

Around the cabin he plowed one shovel at a time, tossing each scoop high above his head, far out away from the log walls until he could not see but ten feet beyond, the snow too high. He found himself at the bottom of a moat, around the back of cabin by the buried wood stacks and onward around reconnecting at the front door. This moat revealed each window of four, each pane intact except for the one he broke into. Having created a clear circumference, he stood in front of the entrance, his back to the mounds, his face smiling in pride at his uncovered hobble.

The daylight had dripped away and his headlamp helped to locate the tarp frozen to the split firewood, this he tore back to reveal the lumber. Into the musk now less he carried 10 armloads of wood. By the stove sat a metal bucket still full of dry kindling, beside this bucket was another full of bark scraps, old moss from the pines, a newspaper dated December 19th, many years ago. He smiled at the date, for the significance it bore. The newspaper he set aside, to read another night, the dry bark, moss and kindling allowed for a fire roaring young and earnest after the lit match spitting sulphur was applied.

The man shed another layer of clothing, his blue fleece faded which for years had served as a pillow too, he draped over a chair, his boots still dragged snow about the cabin, it not melting yet for the floor still clung to the icy world around. Down to just base layers and snow pants, thick padded overalls that hung from hungry shoulders wrapping his body, three well-seasoned logs he placed upon the too hungry kindle, both fire and he the same, famished for life. The fire bellowed with a whoosh as hot air sucked up into the pipe which stood alone for too long, collecting dust and spiders who climbed down from the roof into the lonely abode. For to be an abode one must abode within, knew the spider and the man.

The chair that now bore his fleece he pulled and placed four feet in front of the glowing woodstove. He took his jacket now frozen stiff on the table beneath the broken window and hung it on the left standing corner of the wooden chairs back. It hung in boxed stubborn crisp, as if arms still filled within. Here they would dry, his boots he pulled at and fought with, almost falling upon his backside in the process. After cursing through frozen laces, he submitted to patience; in front of the fire for another minute he stood until the laces could pry apart. Wet boots faced the flame, his socks he slurped off white pruned feet and laid them upon the sitting flat of the chair. Overalls were next. His left arm reaching for action he unclipped the right shoulder first, then the left shoulder, black warm winter shell fell to his knees. He stepped out left foot first then hopped free with his right. They lay crumpled and cold, like a melted man disappeared into the cabin's wooded floor. Naked save for the long underwear he now wore, as tall child in bedtime preparedness he laughed and bellowed and jumped and skipped about the cabin as snow once white upon the brown floor had too now disappeared and lay as puddles soon to be forgotten. He was free! He was home! He was wet and wild with warmth again!

Breath of newborn night shot an icy western blast of snow across the room. The window he had crawled through stood still broken and open. He could not celebrate yet, there was much more work to be done. Clothes lay drying. The stove allowed a gentle glow of light about the cabin, he spotted an incongruent stack of multi-sized scrap wood in the corner. Within this stack was ample supply to build a temporary wooden window, he would live with three-window-walls this winter, three and a door, that would suffice.

He chose five solid boards, longer than wide. In cupboard, a roll of waterproof plastic wrap was stashed, from this he cut a large rectangle swath, enough to bleed well over the edges of the window. Nails were plentiful, sitting in old tin coffee cans by two hammers. With all materials upon the table beneath portal to the cold, beyond the rabbit hole within, he pulled the table into room's center, transitioning the garment-drying chair a tad so the light would bare directly from the glorious singing metal box alive upon his simple project. Two more hands he could use, two sweet feminine hands with fingers to kiss, fingers that grasped not just him but this damn plastic as well, he held the nails in his mouth, first board in his right, the plastic in his left, trying to keep the plastic in place as the wind battered the back, his forearm pressing first board across the open window, a strong gust from the outside and the plastic slapped his face along with the cold, his fingers slipped and the whole ensemble dropped to the ground. Shit. Damn it. He stood back pissed at his idiocrasy. This would not do. His stomach rumbled again. He looked around, finish this then make dinner you idiot, there is a much simpler way. I know you are tired, I know it has been a hell of a journey but this is easy. Get the roofing nails first, slap up the plastic alone then one by one nail the boards on top. Don't make this more difficult on yourself, just stop thinking like a tired idiot, kid. And so, he did. The task simple, his body tired, his adrenaline high. Once complete he stood back proud of the warmth he had created, the cabin now holding its new heat sufficiently. Window now just a part of the wall, no critters to crawl in nor out, no wind to slap his face whilst peeling carrots. Carrots, yes, and onions, garlic, potatoes, and so much more in his pack, it was time to cook dinner.

First from the long cupboard which extended the entire western wall save for the now patched window hole, he pulled out and dusted off two large cooking pots black from the fires of old, a large cast-iron skillet, few ladles and wooden bowls. Into the dark again, through the south facing front door, into his moat beneath the great walls of snow he hustled and packed one ten-gallon pot to the rim with snow and set it next to the glowing woodstove. He would cook his stew in the smaller five-gallon pot and continue to add snow into the ten-gallon until it was full of water for cleaning, cooking and drinking. Many empty plastic jugs were stashed behind the ragged old orange couch in the north-eastern corner of the cabin, these he would fill with treated boiled snowmelt.

The snow melted quickly, condensing and shrinking following gravity's beckon to the bottom of the pot. The man rubbed snowmelt across the entire wooden table, a palate of creation four feet by six, a few carvings donned the top from days afore. A tree, a butterfly, a few flowers, a golden eagle, much more to come he imagined, an incomplete work of art that would allow him to create his newest, thick-hearted mountain stew.

The table was as clean as necessary, dirt is woodland spice after all, and any germs that could survive the cold and the cook would only strengthen his immune system more. To be too clean is not clean at all. He sat his pack upright leaning against the corner leg and began to unload all its edible contents. A large bag of beans, bag of rice, salt and pepper, nine potatoes, a few bulbs of garlic, six onions, much pasta, three pounds of top beef sirloin, a bundle of long orange carrots.

He tossed the carrots upon the couch and laughed. "Where did you go!?" They settled into the dusty gloom of no ass prints. "I am home! I am free! I shall jump on the couch if it please me!" And so, he did.

Next, there was a bag of granola, bag of raisins, bag of prunes, bag of cashews, dried whole milk powder, powder chocolate, a bar of free-trade chocolate, dark almond toffee crunch for a treat on right day, coffee beans, a large block of sharp cheddar cheese, white like the snow, white like the Vermont moonlight over Champlain far away to the east. A few more cans of tuna and red tomato paste to add to the cupboard, another pint of olive oil, another canister of fuel, a long stick of salami, a tightly packed tin of loose tobacco, bag of flour, jar of yeast, a large frozen block of butter, loaf of rustique bread, and sugar both white and brown. Thinking of baking soda, powder, crushed red pepper, Italian seasonings, bay leaves, cayenne, cumin, cilantro, oregano, basil, cardamom and more, he checked his long cupboards again satisfied to see old seasonings of yore. 'That should do until I can freshen my stock', he thought. To finish off his pack unload he dug out a cream of mushroom can, a frozen packet of chicken that had settled to the bottom resting upon his sleeping bag, and finally from within the depths of the cumbersome heavy sack he had carried up the mountain from town through the snow, a brown glorious bottle of bourbon.

The man stood above his table full of food with the bottle in his right hand. Fire-light beamed upon his underweared legs, his butt still slightly damp, hair tangled and matted, his torso now dry, his inners dry too. Water had been his only drink for a month now, the drinking before one of mourn that crumbled into an ill-controlled anger. He did not feel the anger anymore, less the sadness, all was quiet within, for now. The bottle he set beside the onions, and considered. Only for a moment, as he then smiled peacefully. This is a celebration of new, not a lament of old, twisting off the cap he poured three-fingers tall into the tin mug carried for thousands of miles. The tin cup remained cold in the air, he sloshed the brown warmth around then lifted it to his dry lips. The gentle burn soothed his throat, his brain, his empty stomach it told, there is nothing to fear, it shall not remain cold in here.

Upon the table, he first sliced two onions. Then cloves of garlic smashed, peeled clean and diced into small bits, 'til a mountain of garlic and onion filled the bottom of the five-gallon pot. He added two cups of snowmelt water and placed the pot upon the hot iron top of woodstove. The top sirloin he unwrapped and dissected into three one-pound sections, wrapped the remaining two back up then cut one pound into smaller bits. Into the cooking pot the meat went. Four carrots he peeled and sliced, into the pot. Two potatoes he did not peel but cut into fat cubes, this he set aside to be added after the meat had browned. The cream of mushroom he added into the slop along with hearty tablespoons of pepper and salt. The man with butt now finally dry after cold wet day gave the pot many good stirs with a wooden spoon he had carved himself years ago, clockwise and back until it all danced together in one symbiotic jubilee. A bay leaf he tossed into the bustle. Homely scent of onions and garlic strong filled the cabin. Mountain man lifted tin cup to his lips. As he drank the sweet bourbon with a smile and glow, the winter wind howled outside his warm secure cabin.

The food must simmer for some time upon the woodstove; cheese, bread and bourbon would hold him over for now. His clothes upon the chair had now dried, the puddle below the clothes too had dried. Hot embers filled the woodstove inducing any log even damp from before to burst into blue hissing flames. He put only one new piece upon the red sparkling diamonds, the food above did not need a full box of energy, low and slow would allow the stew in the end to be tender, rich with flavor.

In this time with food on simmer, clothes dry and hung, cabin heated and locked down for the night, he sat upon his orange couch and put his feet upon the low table to its front. No trees donned this wooden canvas but a plethora of name carvings and dates of old, quotes of poetic verse, nicknames from his love, friends far away no deader than himself, or more, or less, it did not matter anymore. He set the tin of tobacco and a book of dry rolling papers onto the drunken scratched ancestral slab. It was a good solid table. Two solid tables he had. This pleased him very much as he rolled a smoke and lit it leaning back on his couch, looking about the cabin in glow at its patient trustworthy strength.

He had not yet re-explored all its nooks. In the north-western most corner of the cabin, to the right of his orange lounge, hung a small loft a quarter-size of the main room. A gnarled beam firmly set in the ground held the loft confidently above, above cupboards to the right of now patched window. Beneath the slant of cabin roof lay his bed, a mattress he had constructed from burlap sacks, summer mountain soot and feathers and thread. His blankets surely now torn and filled with mouse droppings or nests. There was no need to function the loft until the following day, tonight the couch would suffice.

He poured the remaining bourbon from tin down throat and dragged upon his smoke. Exhale. After hanging in the air a moment, it meandered its wispy way from his lungs into the mouth of the hot beast, dancing its way down over the flavorful simmer then charging up through the stove pipe into the cold howling night sky through the pines and fir tops, up up up until floating amongst the stars having become nothing but a vapor, molecules apart, skinny in the thin, forever in its nothingness.

A pressing bladder recharged his slumber, he walked south out the front door to relieve himself. His stream just slight yellow, for he had hydrated well throughout the day, it bore a hot hole into the white packed snow of his moat wall. This the deer and lion and fox would know, stay out, Wilder has returned, Wilder is home.

Wilder did not hurry back indoors. He stood barefooted and bold looking up to the myriad of stars beyond the jagged silhouette of tree tops. The same stars he had looked upon from lands afar, from mountains of his youth, from the desert, from the south, with his father in wait for snow owl, from the rooftop of his mother's. Drink the bottle of wine and throw it far, she shall never know for winter will never bring about the baring dirt truth of spring. Oh, but it does, she always knew of the irresponsible decisions made, of the convoluted fuck-it-why-nots of a child. He stood until the stinging heat of freeze saturated his tired bare soles.

Into the warmth, straight to the bottle, tin refilled, stew stirred with but an hour 'til proper supper, a small log applied to the coals rouge, dry socks put back upon feet and moccasins too his late grandfather once stitched, under the couch, still there, stiff and tight from the unworn cold. He sat back onto his orange lounge, pulled out his journal and pen, set them upon his leg-support table filled with the scratches of mates many moons ago. A deer skin that still lay on eastern arm he pulled over his legs; he remembered the days this he chewed, warm Indian Summer days. Wilder slumped staring at the southern wooden wall across the glow until his eyes slid shut, head slumbered left, the log upon flames disintegrated into embers red then white, stew stilled from simmer to cold and the cabin beneath the snow fell asleep once again.

As a Wolf Breathes

www.ingramcontent.com/pod-product-compliance
Lightning Source LLC
Chambersburg PA
CBHW021143090426
42740CB00008B/912